Documents of Protest and Compassion
The Poetry of Walter Bauer

Walter Bauer, a socially committed writer and humanist, emigrated from Germany to Canada in 1952 after becoming disillusioned with social and intellectual developments in Germany. During his progression from dishwasher to university professor, Canada's multicultural outlook allowed him to remain true to himself and loyal to his intellectual heritage, but he died without seeing his humanistic goals fulfilled. While living in Canada he continued to write poetry for a German audience, but this audience ignored him. At the same time he remained unknown to most Canadians, whom he might have reached had he decided at an earlier stage to write in English. His dilemma, typical of that faced by many immigrant writers, is effectively documented in his writings.

Documents of Protest and Compassion offers the first extensive critical assessment of Bauer's considerable poetic oeuvre. In this long-overdue supplement to recent anthologies of Bauer's poetry and essays on his life and work, Angelika Arend draws on Bauer's diaries and letters to reveal the profoundly humane intentions that guided his choice of themes and structures. She shows that social protest and brotherly compassion, shared responsibility and critical self-reflection are Bauer's main thematic fare, which he presented in simple, yet carefully crafted, poetic structures, and explains how these ideas and forms developed or remained constant in light of historical, cultural, social, and personal developments.

Documents of Protest and Compassion is important for those interested in Bauer's work, German poetry, German-Canadian literature, and the immigrant writing experience.

ANGELIKA AREND is associate professor of German, University of Victoria.

Walter Bauer

"'Wer sich bewegt, berührt die Welt, und wer ruht,
den berührt sie. Deswegen müssen wir immer bereit
sein, zu berühren und berührt zu werden.' (Goethe)
(Tagebuch, 24. Mai 1958)

Documents of Protest and Compassion

The Poetry of Walter Bauer

ANGELIKA AREND

McGill-Queen's University Press
Montreal & Kingston · London · Ithaca

Legal deposit fourth quarter 1999
Bibliothèque nationale du Québec

Printed in Canada on acid-free paper

This book has been published with the help of a grant
from the Humanities and Social Sciences Federation of
Canada, using funds provided by the Social Sciences
and Humanities Research Council of Canada.
Additional funding was provided by the University
of Victoria.

Canada

McGill-Queen's University Press acknowledges the
financial support of the Government of Canada
through the Book Publishing Industry Development
Program (BPIDP) for its activities. We also
acknowledge the support of the Canada Council for
the Arts for our publishing program.

Canadian Cataloguing in Publication Data

Arend, Angelika, 1942–
    Documents of protest and compassion: the poetry of
    Walter Bauer
    Includes bibliographical references and index.
    ISBN 0-7735-1879-7
    1. Bauer, Walter, 1904–1976. – Criticism and
    interpretation. I. Title.
    PT2603.A79Z58 1999   831'.914   C99-900807-2

Typeset in Palatino 10/12
by Caractéra inc., Quebec City

Contents

Acknowledgments

The initial impulse for this study came from Walter Riedel whose continued critical comment and encouragement I acknowledge with gratitude and appreciation. I am equally grateful to Rodney Symington whose constructive criticism and practical help have been invaluable to me. Sincere thanks also to Henry Beissel whose Bauer publications furnished the live wire connecting me to the poet's mind and heart.

I would like to thank Inez Weston and Julian Manyoni for their careful scrutiny of the entire manuscript; Ulrich Profitlich for making available from his archive Walter Bauer's photograph; and Susan Mackey for stepping in at the eleventh hour to discipline the computer that had defeated me.

I wish to acknowledge with thanks permission to quote from Bauer's works granted by the following persons and publishers: Günter Hess: *Lebenslauf*, Unpublished Letters and Diaries; Andreas J. Meyer, Merlin Verlag: *Ein Jahr, Fragment vom Hahnenschrei*; Suhrkamp Verlag: *Geburt des Poeten*; Ragnar Tessloff, Tessloff Verlag: *Der Weg zählt, Klopfzeichen, Mein blaues Oktavheft*.

This book has been published with the help of a grant from the Humanities and Social Sciences Federation of Canada. Additional publication assistance was received from the University of Victoria. I acknowledge both grants with gratitude.

I dedicate this book to Horst Schreiner whose unflagging good humour and support enabled me to complete the project.

Abbreviations

Documents of Protest and Compassion

Introduction

"Wer nichts wegwirft,
macht sein Leben zum Museum."

It seems sadly ironic that a prolific writer such as Walter Bauer, who spent his life in unswerving literary service to his fellow human beings, "brothers" and "friends," should be virtually forgotten in his native Germany, and little known in Canada where he took up residence at age forty-eight. Commentators, small as their number has been to date, have offered plausible explanations. Prior to his emigration in 1952, Bauer had been a well established author – but one among many, one whose poetic voice did not stand out from the general chorus (Maczewski, *Wanderer* 131). Bauer left Germany when intellectual and literary developments were moving in a direction he could no longer follow. He was prompted by a measure of guarded optimism that the distance thus gained might safeguard the integrity of his poetic work:

More and more, and weighing on my mind to the point of despair, I felt I was moving towards a dead end. What I believed in and considered right seemed almost ridiculous when I saw how all over West Germany the old political and "intellectual" forces, which we never wanted to see again, occupied their positions with innocent faces and as if confirmed by history ... I could no longer bear to see how spurious values were hysterically overrated ... I saw myself caught in a net of papery literature production. I couldn't breathe any more. At the end of these reflections I considered it beneath my dignity to end up in this stifling atmosphere as an embittered old writer scribbling into sand. I wanted to rescue for myself a few truths I had found the hard way, and for which I had paid my share.[1]

Inevitably, the courageous step Bauer took cost him dearly. It simply widened the gulf between him and his readers (Beissel, UPM 172). He ended up writing not even in sand but in a vacuum. Within

Canada, his continued use of German drastically reduced the number of potential readers and precluded his entry into the wider literary scene. Bauer found himself in the grip of the typical "immigrant writer's dilemma": isolation both from the people whose native language he shared and from those among whom he lived (Beissel, DS vi). His intended readers in Germany were drifting away on different intellectual currents and had no ear for his "old-fashioned" ideas and concerns. Publishers simply shrugged him off: "Bauer just doesn't sell any more" (UPM 172). During the 1960s, he managed to get into print two slim volumes of poetry (*Klopfzeichen,* 1962; *Fragment vom Hahnenschrei,* 1966), and one volume of selected poetry and prose (*Der Weg zählt, nicht die Herberge,* 1964).[2]

Not everyone agreed with the publishers' verdict. Some of those whose judgment was not swayed by market forces but informed by an intimate knowledge of poetry had something quite different to say. Karl Krolow for one, commenting on the poems contained in *Klopfzeichen,* lauded in no uncertain terms their "healthy dryness," "literary decency" and unabashed "self-sufficiency" that rest on a fine balance of laconic recording and poetic intensity. "How encouraging that such writing still exists in these times of thoroughly intellectualized lyric production," Krolow observed in 1963.[3] Five years later, Hans-Albert Walter concluded his very fair review of *Ein Jahr* with these thoughts: "Surely, it is comforting to know that such a calm and sensible man is still writing in the language that reaches us. After all, we need voices like this one, now more than before."[4] On the occasion of Bauer's death, Rudolf Hagelstange, in his "Word in Memory of Walter Bauer," maintained that in spite of his emigration, Bauer had always remained a German writer who might eventually succeed in "re-immigrating for good."[5] The hope here expressed seems to have been genuine.

The process of Bauer's "re-immigration" may indeed have begun. It was no doubt initiated by Hans-Martin Pleßke's tireless efforts, which led to the reissue of *Stimme aus dem Leunawerk* by Reclam (Leipzig) in 1980. Receptive young minds who had never heard of Walter Bauer welcomed with enthusiasm the "incredible sensitivity and precision ... of these small works that open the reader's heart to thoughts of brotherhood and solidarity" (Trampe).[6] Jürgen Jankofsky, fellow enthusiast and writer, recently gave us an account of the interesting developments here set in motion (*Wanderer* 163–8).

Back in Canada, poet and friend Henry Beissel undertook to promote Bauer as "Canada's immigrant poet par excellence" (DS v), making some of his poetry available in English translation (*The Price of Morning,* 1968; *A Different Sun,* 1976). Literary criticism was quick to point out that the immigrant writer Walter Bauer, who attempted "to continue *from Canada* his literary career in Germany while at the same time expressing disgust with German history and society," was in fact a typically alienated exile caught in a state of "perpetual crisis" (Symington, *Wanderer* 210). Turning the critical tide in Canada too, a collection of essays on Bauer's life and work was published by Walter Riedel and Rodney Symington to mark the ninetieth anniversary of Bauer's birthday (*Der Wanderer*, 1994). A wealth of information and insight has been brought together in this pioneer work whose express purpose it is to rescue this "important author" from undeserved oblivion, "to throw light on his works from various points of view and to present in his true colours this unjustly forgotten writer" (Riedel).[7]

Bauer himself was acutely aware of being forgotten, but he never gave up. What kept him going was a deep-seated hope that sometime, somewhere, someone might hear and appreciate what he had to say. He had in mind "a young person, unknown, who/one day perhaps might read what I wrote" ("Interview with an Elderly Man").[8] This hope may have been fuelled by a sense of consolation drawn from the time-honoured idea of the poet's ennobling isolation from the conforming crowd, as suggested by the story told in the poem, "Die Drosseln sterben nicht aus" (*LL* 95–7). When, after years of unrecognized and unrewarded toil, Bauer found occasion to prepare a selection of his poetry, he executed the task with the seriousness and care of a man who fully comprehended the importance of the opportunity that had presented itself. As it turned out, the resulting volume, titled *Lebenslauf* (1975), did not do much to end Bauer's isolation. To the literary historian, however, and the general reader interested in the poetic work of this "Deutschen in der Welt," as Bauer styled himself (*EJ* 8), this anthology presents a useful selection of poems dating from the beginning of Bauer's literary career in 1929 up to two years prior to his death in 1976. In the space of 124 pages it gathers together what the poet himself considered the best fruits of his lifelong lyric endeavour in his mother tongue. While the value judgment underlying the poet's personal selection remains as subjective as any informed critic's choice, it affords insight into the poet's own perspective and adds an extra dimension to our understanding and evaluation of his poetry.

The title *Lebenslauf* is both characteristic and apt. First, it is expressive of Bauer's keen interest in the lives of people past and present, as evidenced by his various prose portraits of artists and other great men,[9] and by the host of poems reflecting on the turns, predicaments, visible and hidden wrinkles in the lives of fellow humans around him. Secondly, the chronological sequence of the poems brought together in this volume guides the reader along the course of Bauer's own creative life. By his own testimony, writing meant being alive: "In the morning I wrote a few lines. Regardless of whether they are good or bad ... to me they are breaths of air ["Atemzüge"], and to know that I am breathing, still breathing, makes me happy."[10] Over the years, the exercise of such "breathing" resulted in an uninterrupted account of the poet's "Lebenslauf," which the anthology *Lebenslauf* now offers in representative selection.

Bauer's poetic account of his life is divided into two parts that group together poems written before and after his emigration. Part One spans twenty-six years (1926 to 1952); it comprises thirty-seven poems which may be subdivided into four thematic groups along the lines of German history as Bauer witnessed it from the days of his childhood: World War I, the years of industrialization and the depression, the Nazi era and World War II, and the postwar years. Part Two contains forty-one poems written during the two decades between 1952 and 1972. Finding himself outside the coordinates of European history, the poet now speaks with a more personal voice, either dealing with issues of his immediate experience, observation, and thinking: emigration and immigration, autobiographical reflections, life at the university; or reflecting more generally on human beings in the world that surrounds them: social, political, and ethical concerns, art and the *condition humaine*. In the present study, chapters 2 and 3 are devoted to the preemigration poems Bauer gathered in Part One of his *Lebenslauf*, chapters 4 to 7 to the poems written in Canada and gathered in Part Two.

Henry Beissel informs us that Bauer left behind "a welter of poems" (about 600) that have remained unpublished, a good number of which had been prepared for publication in three book-length manuscripts (see UPM 169ff). Towards the end of his life, Bauer had also begun to write poetry in English, "a handful," as Beissel puts it (UPM 194), eight of which were published posthumously in a special issue of *The Tamarack Review* in 1979. A selection of these late poems, in both German and English, will be discussed in chapter 8. A synopsis of Bauer's views on poetry (chapter 1) will preface the chronological review, a short postscript will conclude it.

CHAPTER ONE

Poetic Creed

✌ *"Man muß einen 'record' zurücklassen.*
Etwas wie: ich war bei euch, und das its mein
Bericht."

Before entering into a discussion of Bauer's poetry, one needs to find out what he himself thought about the motives, mechanisms, and purpose of his lyrical endeavour. He did not write any programmatic piece that neatly sums it all up, but as a dedicated diarist he put down on paper numerous relevant comments and reflections, and as a university lecturer he published an essay on "German Poetry Today" (1965) in which he laid down the salient points of his own position. The following presentation is based principally on his published volume of *"Tagebuchblätter,"* titled *Ein Jahr* (1967), and the above mentioned essay of 1965.

For Bauer writing meant breathing, that is: being alive. The poet cannot help but exercise his craft, regularly, incessantly. It is an involuntary life giving activity, the awareness of which enhances appreciation of life. By Bauer's own account, this urge must have been with him at a very early age; at fourteen he "had already filled whole exercise books, poems, dramatic scenes."[1] It may safely be assumed that one motive force of this urge to write was an innate "Formulierungsfreude," a pleasure derived from consciously using and putting together words. In the moving little volume *Geburt des Poeten,* from which I have just quoted, there is a telling anecdote: "And so I said to my mother ... I was man enough. I said 'man enough' because I had read this expression somewhere and I liked it; back home they often laughed about the words I used ... 'Now listen to this,' my mother said, 'this titch, and the kind of German he's speaking, like a preacher,' and she laughed and pulled the old hat I was wearing over my face."[2]

The creative process itself is sparked off in an apparently sudden moment of inspiration and is experienced as an intensely physical act. Again, an anecdote will serve to illuminate: "In the meadowland near Merseburg, at dusk, it was dripping from the sky, line by line. – The moon has had a good rest after her last journey/She is rising, round like a bubble blown from a mouth … I ran home to write it down, at the kitchen table. The lump in the throat [also in English in the original] – it has forever remained like this, even when I wrote such things as 'When We Conquer the Universities' … Naive? I admit it."[3]

To justify such seeming "naiveté," Bauer calls to witness accredited practitioners such as Goethe, Benn, Wallace Stevens, and Jiminez, all of whom have rendered testimony to this effect (EJ 171). What he rejects emphatically is the idea promoted by some contemporary poets and editors that the writing of a poem is done purely on the basis of distanced calculation and design: "Even Brecht cannot tell me he was cool as a cucumber when he wrote verses. I am a little suspicious when poets give long lectures on the production of a poem. – 'My Poem Is a Knife,' was the title of a book, it was almost ridiculous to see how gifted people wrote only of coldness, of intention, of design; similar things are done by young poets, not the best, in East Germany."[4] The book here criticized is Hans Bender's famous anthology Mein Gedicht ist mein Messer of 1961; and the young poets referred to were those writing (or having to write) according to the doctrine of Socialist Realism.

In another context Bauer talks about "being moved" ("Ich bin bewegt," LL 12), a condition of mind and body that both initiates and propels the creation of a poem. He hastens to add, however, that "work and revision" will follow as part of the overall process: "First you are moved, then follow work and revision of this work."[5] His relevant diary entry says much the same, only with greater emotional intensity: "Naturally a poem is not a gift from Heaven – old hat, what you are saying here – it is work."[6] Indeed, the twin formula of inspiration and perspiration, energy and reason, is nothing new and Bauer only adds to the long list of similar observations by fellow practitioners past and present.

Important for us is his emphatic acknowledgment of the emotive/somatic aspect of the creative process. He rejects passionately the idea, fashionable since Gottfried Benn's influential lecture on "Problems of Lyric Poetry" (1951), that the composition of a poem is in essence "laboratory work." The results show, Bauer argues, obsession with descriptive detail can only produce lifeless artifacts: "How come that modern literature does not know any more the taste of bread and simple things? They describe, precisely, precisely to a fault, but it lacks fragrance, it's laboratory."[7] The simple, elementary things in life, their taste, their smell, have been banished from this kind of writing: "Food and drink and the pleasure of eating and drinking are hardly ever mentioned in today's literature ... There's no time for eating and drinking. They are too busy rummaging through the absurdities of life ... Don't they ever eat? Don't they ever drink? Don't they ever belch? No. Life is too absurd."[8]

This biting criticism is a measure of Bauer's impatience with contemporary intellectualism which, in his view, had lost sight of the base where life is lived and was unduly engrossed in life's absurdities. It is only consistent that Bauer should take aim at New Criticism as well and accuse it of being engaged in an "esoterische Ausflucht" (EJ 138). To him, this school's preoccupation with the artistic makeup of "the well-wrought urn" was tantamount to "gingerly dipping one's toes into the stream of life of which literature forms part."[9] Such an approach remains outside the genuine artist's realm of experience and creative practice: "One day, you sticklers for detail, one must stop counting the waves of the river to find out what the river is. That is the moment the artist is born: he walks through the river or swims in it and says: water, earth, river, sky."[10]

The poet, as Bauer sees him, immerses himself in authentic experience and makes an authentic effort at authentic expression: "Apply yourselves in your own way. Reject cheap solutions. Be authentic."[11] Fashionably "beautiful" poetry can never be his goal: "Lines by a Swiss poet. All the same handwriting. Sentimentality of soberness; that too can become a pose. How long can one speak in a low voice? Language possesses pride, joy, wings. One day the prayer-and-repentance-day mentality must be cast aside – beauty is not calligraphy."[12]

What such "calligraphy" lacks is the all–important ingredient of down-to-earth humaneness: "Das Menschliche entscheidet," Bauer quotes from Rosa Luxemburg's letters, adding the significant explanation that these are letters to *friends* (EJ 34). Another diary entry discusses this point in some detail: "It is true: during the past twenty years German poets have rediscovered the miracle of existence. But it seems to me that in this discovery something is missing almost entirely – let us call it: fellow human, friend, brother; let us call the feeling friendship, friendliness, sympathy. Poetry that does not include the human being may sparkle and be boldly experimental; but it will be devoid of the essence; in the end it will cease to be poetry."[13]

Clearly, these words are aimed at the type of poetry advocated by Gottfried Benn and his disciples. Benn, incidentally, had also been critical of the current wave of existentialism and had dismissed it, with his own sharp tongue, as "de[n] ganze[n] Rummel des Existentialismus" (*Ausgewählte Briefe* 173). Bauer's gentler disposition moved him to couch his criticism in softer tones, pointing to the absence on the contemporary scene of words that would indicate the all-important presence of the caring gesture of one human being to another. Ultimately, Bauer argues, humanism – the essence of life – also forms the essence of poetry.

Humanism is what moves the poet Bauer, collector of "alles, was um mich ist," to give preference to "Blicke, Berührungen, Stimmen" (*EJ* 80); to reach out to the "Menschen des Alltags" (*EJ* 207); to defend the cause of the "heart": "Today so many people are so clever. They know so much that in the end they don't know where the heart is."[14] And: "Goethe believed in the human heart. Did not Brecht too – in spite of everything?"[15] The company of famous writers, which Bauer by the evidence of his diaries liked to invoke, seems reassuring, if somewhat overwhelming. "The great writers never departed from reality; they discovered humanity even in a dog," he concludes, admitting to that familiar "lump in the throat" at the thought of it.[16]

Portrayal and promotion of *Menschlichkeit*, then, is what the poet's task is all about. He has no "message," no handy moral, religious, or ideological formula: "The relationship of many Germans to their writers is thoroughly wrong, because it is not natural. They expect messages – instead of listening to a worker in his field saying to them: this is what I have tried to do."[17] What this "field worker" may indeed have to pass on is "light," which he receives in the process of his endeavours: "The awakening of the poet is the awakening of the first flush of dawn. He takes the light in his hand and distributes it fairly ... Just distribution of light is easy. Just distribution of bread is far more difficult. To do this, you may, depending on circumstances, have to risk your neck."[18]

"Light" can mean many different things, including "enlightenment," both temporal and spiritual. The time honoured notion of the poet as mediator, minister, priest does not seem to be far away. Bauer here makes a distinction between service to the people on a mental/ psychological plane ("light") and service on a physical/social plane ("bread"), implying clearly that the latter is not rendered by the poet. This is a veiled but nonetheless clear "No" to those who wished to utilize literature for sociopolitical ends – the Marxists of different kinds in both Germanys of Bauer's time.

As Hans-Martin Pleßke explains, Bauer envisioned "die Veränderung der Welt vom Seelischen her" (*Wanderer* 44). Any effort to "change the world" would have to emanate not from a material but from a mental/spiritual source. The following diary entry throws light on the workings of the process: "Art is alchemy; chemistry on a higher plane. It extends the process of life and sublimates it … people act on each other like acids, salts, and sulphur; everything acts on everything; in this process the substance of human life is transformed and heightened. It is prepared in sorrow, in wisdom, in love."[19] What the poet has thus processed and refined is sent out in the hope that it may reach and affect receptive minds and hearts.

In sum, Bauer's conception of poetry, while declining to serve any social or political agenda, is essentially communicative. It espouses "Lyrik für Leser," (Hage 3–18), which offers an account of what one person "sah und aufnahm, dachte und fühlte" (LL 12): "One must leave behind a 'record.' Something like: I was among you, and this is my report."[20] The poet who undertakes to write such an account will have to face, not to forget, history, he will "have to throw off the mask of out-worn fashionable nihilism [and] renounce the bankrupt theme of decay, decline, of the separation of the artist from his fellow men" ("German Poetry Today" 225). He will do so to "work towards a new vision of man" in order ultimately to "restore the face of man" (225).

The poetic language equal to this task will steer clear of the "more or less traditional and trivial … sentimentalism" rampant in East German poetry and "the preciousness and affectation" debilitating its West German counterpart: "To retreat into magic darkness has become more or less cheap escapism and is no longer authentic. The play with verbal magic and opaque symbolism can now be played by gifted high-school students. Turgid loquacity covers too often an impoverished heart; so does carefully constructed understatement. There are too many poets whose first name is Narcissus … There is too little compassion for the fellow man, too much inflated mysticism, too much self-pity." (224)

The poet whom Bauer hails as exemplar and model is, above all, Bertolt Brecht, "who asked in a precise way the question of the values and the validity of life. He gave … a model of simple unaffected poetic language which had strength and delicacy, hardness and tenderness and which was a means of human communication" (217). In the following chapters I shall examine whether and, if so, to what extent and in what manner, Walter Bauer succeeded in writing poetry that meets the standard set by his chosen model.

> *"Für welche Ernte?*
> *Mut … wir hoffen …"*

Since the medium forms a good part of the message, I now turn to Bauer's poetry and examine some thematically relevant poems. This enquiry will offer the added benefit of chronology, affording insight into changes, modifications or shifts of emphasis that occurred in the course of Bauer's lifelong endeavour. In view of his life-oriented humanism it comes as no surprise that he has devoted a relatively small portion of his extensive body of poetry to reflections on poetry. What he has written on the topic seems to highlight major points in his writing career, indicating also a tendency towards growing restraint as years and experiences accumulate.

In Bauer's first two volumes of poetry there are two poems relevant to this enquiry: "Anruf" (KS [1929] 48–9) is an explanatory appeal by the poet to the "comrades" for whom he is writing; "An die kommenden Dichter" (SL [1930] 123–4) is a poet's call to the young generation of poets, detailing do's and don'ts of their task. Making allowance for the energy and passion only the young writer could muster, one is easily persuaded by the eloquent evidence of these poems that Bauer was Bauer right from the start, or conversely, that Bauer remained consistently true to himself.

The "Genossen Dichter" addressed in the latter poem are people sensitive to the burning issues of their time: "die Funken der brennenden Zeit [fallen ihnen] in die Augen" (st. I, line 12). They are thus "moved" – to use Bauer's later expression – to render testimony to the "Leidenschaft des Herzens" (st. I, line 15), to experiencing "Ergriffenheit" (st. I, line 16). Their whole-hearted involvement rules out any wasteful attention to the beauty of form or rhyme, any concern for originality or aesthetic appropriateness, any escape into the irrelevancy of nature poetry:

> Laßt euch nicht irremachen von denen, die euch vorwerfen:
> Pathos, Nachahmung –
> wenn wir singen, so ist vielleicht die Form aus dem vorigen Jahrhundert,
> aber das Herz ist von 1930. (St. II, lines 8–11)

> Singt nicht die Kornfelder des Sommers, die Sense nicht,
> überlaßt den Gesang der Landschaften
> (wenn sie noch da sind)
> denen, die nach euch kommen,
> wenn sie es für wert halten, von Landschaften zu singen. (St. III)

Being grounded in their own time, the poets are to give voice to the "Geräusche" of their own time:

> Jeder Mensch erhebt sich auf dem Grund seiner Zeit,
> ihr, Genossen Dichter, erhebt euch
> auf dem Grund vergangener Schlacht,

unermeßlichen Todes.

...

also sollen sie aussprechen den unermeßlichen Tod, die
Geräusche unserer Zeit. (St. iv)

All this the mature Bauer was to condense in the two–word for-
mula "seid authentisch." Such authentic writing forms an integral
part of life, requiring neither extra time nor a special place; it is done,
"wo es euch einfällt, wo die Zeit euch brennt" (st. vii, line 1), be it
on a bench in the city park or in a streetcar (st. vii, line 3). This
recalls the boy running home to write at the kitchen table.

The things thus put to paper are to serve as "signals of alarm," as
"flares along the roads into the sloughs of despair," as "reports of the
daily battle":

Signale des Alarms, wenn die Kolonnen zusammenfallen,
Leuchtfeuer an den Wegen in die Sümpfe der Verzweiflung

...

Berichte aus der täglichen Schlacht,
in die Gehirne zu hämmern! (St. v, lines 2–3; 5–6)

The words "Leuchtfeuer" and "Berichte" are significant. The
former seems to be an early harbinger of Bauer's later notion of the
poet's light-mediating function. In the present poem, the idea of the
poet as mediator, as receiver and giver, is rendered by an auricular
image: "Ihr! Hörrohre, gestellt in das Unendliche, / sprecht aus die
Bewegungen der Zeit, singt Aufruf und Tat!" (st. viii, lines 1–2)
What these "junge Genossen Dichter" (st. viii, line 3) "hear" they
will transform into speech and song, which again will be heard and
transformed, this time into action.

The word "Berichte" likewise anticipates an idea central to Bauer's
thinking, even though the present rather more aggressive context of
political agitation speaks of "reports of the daily battle, / to be ham-
mered into people's brains!" (st. v, lines 5–6) Such revolutionary fer-
vour did not last, but the idea of poets writing "reports" rather than
"vollendete Dichtung" ("Anruf," line 3) did. While the young poet
saw fit to state explicitly, "Wir notieren das Leben" ("Anruf," line 7),
the mature poet invoked the suggestive power of a "Leerstelle" ("Ich
war hier") is the terse sum total of his life, inviting the perceptive
reader to fill in: "meine Dichtung ist mein Bericht" ("Interview mit
einem älteren Mann," FH 98: xvii, lines 4 and 10).

In "Anruf" we also find, rendered typically as a caring gesture from
one brother to another, an explanation of what the poet aims to do.
It is to shake his "brother" into realizing and accepting his "affection,"

into seeing the world with open eyes, into sharing the suffering of his fellow men, into leadership if possible, certainly into fellowship and truly being "part of the world":

> Bruder, daß du erschüttert bist wie wir,
> daß du hinfällst und dich aufrichtest
> an unsrer Zuneigung,
> wir würden sonst schweigen;
> daß du siehst, Bruder, daß du deine Augen aufreißt,
> daß du mit-leidend wirst
> und vorangehst, wann du vorangehen kannst.
> Und willst du nicht, geh unter uns,
> wir stützen dich.
> Welche Stimme du singst, bist du
> der zärtliche Geliebte, bist Genosse du
> ...
> nur: daß du wahrhaftig singst und ein Teil der Welt – (Lines 8–21)

The young communist's zestful sense of mission clearly was the cradle of the mature humanist's more subdued, yet unbroken desire to reach out, touch, and move.

One last comment on the young Bauer's advice to "die kommenden Dichter":

> Ihr müßt euch gefaßt machen
> auf Unverständnis und Einsamkeit,
> weil ihr verzichtet auf die Glätte,
> weil ihr Kameraden der Zeit sein wollt. (St. vi)

Being true "comrades of your time" may mean having to go against the smooth grain of conventional expectations, and to face lack of understanding and loneliness. This, of course, is an idea with a long tradition. It nevertheless seems prophetic of Bauer's own painful experience during the latter part of his life. The poem "Die Drosseln sterben nicht aus" (LL 95–7) is there to tell the story. Written about three decades later in the solitude of Bauer's Toronto apartment, it draws the ultimate conclusion of the poet's otherness. Not only is he excluded from society, he is actually hounded down and killed by the "Neun-bis-fünf-Männer" and their "braven Hausfrauen" (st. I). Years later, a scholar discovers a dead poet and brings out his works (st. II). Eventually a monument is erected in his honour and the speaker's edifying words serve to elevate the hearts of all (st. III). The monument is soon forgotten (st. IV), but sometime later a young person hits upon the dead poet's verses and recognizes the voice of a "friend" and mentor:

> Ja, er ist mein guter Freund, ich will
> Ihm folgen, ich will
> Singen, ich will
> Kein Neun-bis-fünf-Mann sein.
> Ah, mein toter Freund, rief er,
> Wie hell wird die Welt durch dich. (St. v, lines 7–12)

Society once again swings into action to hound down this young enthusiast, too (st. vi), but as the concluding two-line section assures us, poets do not die out (st. vii).

It is hard not to read this piece autobiographically. Bauer clearly takes aim at the "Wirtschaftswunder–Gesellschaft" he decided to leave before being "erdrosselt" ("strangled"). His bitterness, however, is tempered by the hope that one day his work will reach and inspire those persons, if only a few, unmarred by the ways of the society that drove him into exile. It was this hope which kept his pen going in spite of the debilitating effect of solitude. This inference is confirmed by a passage found in the even more overtly autobiographical "Interview mit einem älteren Mann" of 1966 where Bauer uses almost identical words. I have quoted from this passage before; here it is in full:

> Manchmal [denke ich] an einen jungen Menschen, unbekannt, der
> Eines Tages vielleicht lesen wird, was ich schrieb,
> Um zu sagen: Den Mann hätte ich gern gekannt,
> Vielleicht wäre er mein Freund geworden.
> Ich bin schon sein Freund und hoffe auf ihn. (FH 92: IX, lines 11–15)

The ring of assurance may be deceptive. The short poem "Weißes Blatt war wie ein Feld" (KN [1962] 22), allows us a glimpse of a sense of uncertainty that must have visited the everbusy poet now and then. This poem depicts him in the company of himself, whom he "meets" at night (line 1), filling the sheet of paper in front of him with words "saturated with hope." The opening comparison of paper to field and words to seeds is modified at the end:

> Weißes Blatt war wie ein Feld, in dem ich
> Schreibend langsam Furchen zog,
> Und die Worte fielen wie Saatkörner, lautlos,
> Getränkt mit Hoffnung. (Lines 1–4)

Und wie er beuge ich mich wieder zum Blatt
Wie einem Schneefeld, das auf die Saathand wartet. (Lines 14–15)

The field is a snow field waiting for the sower's hand – "Für welche Ernte? / Und wir lächeln einander zu: Mut ... wir hoffen" lines 16–17). What chance of survival and growth is there for seeds planted in snow?

Four years later, a similar image was to serve as the vehicle of a rather more determined sense of purpose. Under the telling title "Narrheit? Hoffnung?" (FH 102), the poet confesses to having undertaken constructive work precisely at the moment when war was imminent, and destruction a distinct possibility:

Als vom Krieg gesprochen wurde,
Plante ich schönere, festere Häuser.
Als die Wolken sich zusammenzogen,
Fing ich zu bauen an.
Morgen kann alles ausgelöscht werden,
Ich weiß: ich war Zeuge und Teilnehmer. (St. 1)

In the same vein, "this evening" – night is imminent – he will undertake to write, on a piece of paper whose whiteness encourages him to do so, "of the good things in this world":

Doch heute abend
Schimmert das Blatt,
Auf dem ich von den guten Dingen der Welt
Schreiben will,
Wie unbetretener Schnee. (St. 11)

In spite of better knowledge and past experience he decides to ignore the bad and focus on the good.

This, if anything, is the "message" of Bauer's poetry which is informed by a deep love of people in spite of their many erroneous ways. As Bauer explained one year before his death, what had moved and carried him through the greater part of his creative life was "active scepticism which for all its knowledge of the possibilities and impossibilities of human nature is softened by carefully weighing sympathy."[21] The source of his creative energy was his conviction "that there is more to admire about the human being than there is to despise; even if sometimes I have to bite my tongue."[22] This calls to mind the diary entry attesting to Bauer's overriding interest in things human – "Blicke, Berührungen, Stimmen." The poem "Flüsse sah ich" (published in 1962: KN 61) offers graphic detail. While the sound of rivers flowing across the earth put the speaking "I" to sleep, tears on human faces made him alert and excited his interest (st. I); while veins of gold running through the earth did touch some sensitive chords in him, they were forgotten at the sight of the veins in his mother's hands (st. II); the song of green forests impressed him in its greatness, but human laughter spelled happiness to him (st. III): "In Gesichtern war ich zu Haus" (st. III, line 6).

The lesson one may derive from this: do not look for much nature poetry in Bauer's œuvre. While in his young years he had been impelled by his revolutionary fervour to throw nature poetry overboard, his mature stance was beyond such uncompromising rejection. But his preference for the human landscape is clear from the copious evidence of "Lebensläufe," "Bildnisse," renderings of encounters and reflections on human affairs. His poetry teems with people, men and women, young and old, many foreign, most ordinary and some extraordinary, suffering and persevering, learning and teaching, forgetting, forgiving, etc. etc. – all seen through the filter of the poet's compassionate eye.

A summary of what he considered essential to the task of presenting this human kaleidoscope may be gleaned from the poem "Postkarte an junge Poeten," published in mid-career (NT [1957] 92). This fictitious "Sendschreiben," to borrow Martin Luther's fitting label, serves the poet to give voice and, by means of amplification, rein to his impatience with his young colleagues whose misguided efforts invite nothing but rejection – rejection by the arcana they seek, impelled by their wrongheaded desire to impress their readers with profundity that no one possesses:

> Ihr sucht das Unverständliche auf, um es unverständlich auszudrücken,
> Das Geheimnis, das ihr so wenig versteht, wie alle, ist euch
> begehrenswerter als das Tägliche.
> Das Geheimnis verwirft euch. (St. I)

They are rejected by nature which they observe poorly and render in ineffectual images:

> Mit beschlagenen Brillen belauscht ihr die Natur, um falsche
> Bilder zu finden, an denen sich niemand entzückt,
> Weil keiner sie versteht.
> Die Natur verwirft euch. (St. II)

They are rejected also by time, whose present reality they ignore in favour of future gloom and doom:

> Ihr lebt in Aeonen, mit denen wir nichts anfangen können, weil wir heute
>   leben,
> Klagt über kommenden Untergang mit bewölkter Stirn und schreit nach
>   Ruhm und Hilfe,
> ...
> Ihr verachtet die Zeit, und so weiß die Zeit nichts von euch.
> Die Zeit verwirft euch. (St. III, lines 1–2; 4–5)

They are rejected by life which their complacent paper knowledge can comprehend neither in its personal nor in its political dimensions:

> Ihr vermeidet, von Lagern zu sprechen, von endloser Flucht, von Bürger-
>   kriegen,
> Über Diktatoren und Barbarei lächelt ihr smart,
> ...
> Ihr kennt weder Rausch noch Fluch noch Umarmung.
> Euch gehört nichts als Papier.
> Das Leben verwirft euch. (St. IV, lines 2–3; 6–8)

To put it positively, the main pillars of Bauer's poetic programme, as displayed here, are accessibility of subject matter and clarity of expression, keen observation and appropriate imagery, contemporaneity and, most important, relevance born of authentic experience of life.

As both Bauer's diary and the poem "Keine Botschaften, kein Aufruf" (NT 47) show, none of this is to serve as a vehicle for any superior wisdom, or as a call to action aiming to change the world:

> Keine Botschaften, kein Aufruf
> Zur Veränderung der Welt –
> ...
> Ein paar einfache Dinge nur:
> ...
> Am Grunde sieht man die Dinge des Grundes. (Lines 1–2; 8; 17)

All of this is to serve the expression of human life lived without undue claims and aspirations which indeed is apt to open our eyes to the things that matter.

Everyone is capable of such insights, but not everyone possesses the gift to express and communicate them. Here lie the true task and the responsibility of the poet. Just how seriously these were embraced by Walter Bauer may be gauged from the moving "Anruf" – yes: to God – which he wrote at the time when the people he loved so deeply had reached the lowest point on the scale of human experience. The year was 1947. A few lines will suffice.

Gib mir das Wort –
nicht für mich – für alle, die leiden.
...
Laß mich das Wort finden, das jeden berührt,
das feurige, zarte, das stille und brausende Wort.
...
Wort, das wie Quellwasser der Berge schmeckt und den
Durstigen erfrischt, das dem Einsamen wie eine gute
Berührung auf der Schulter ist, ihn getröstet aufblicken
läßt aus den Schlammfeldern und Brackwassern der Welt.

(DT 7, lines 1–2; 13–14; 18–21)

The word that speaks to, moves, and consoles everyone is nothing short of impossible. Bauer knew it, of course, and relied on the intimacy of a prayer and the urgency of the historical hour to explain and excuse the grand ambition here formulated.

The idea fundamental to Bauer's poetic creed – the idea that poetry should be an authentic "record" which possesses the power to speak effectively to its reader – raises a number of questions. Do the material factualness, the objectivity, and emotional detachment of a "record" or "account" make for powerful poetic discourse? Does Bauer's own poetry bear out his idea of poetic recording? Does it measure up to his demand for precision and simplicity, strength, and delicacy? What textual strategies and artistic devices does it employ to speak to and involve its reader? Do its basic patterns remain constant or do they change over the years? These questions will provide the main focus of the following examination of Walter Bauer's poetry as selectively represented in his last volume, *Lebenslauf.*

The Old World ...

"Aber ich
brenne nach der Welt, wie sie ist,
sich darbietet dem ersten Blick,
dem Herzen ..."
                              ("Arbeiter und Student," 1930: SL 80)

Mastering the Craft

⚜ *"Schreibt, wo es euch einfällt,*
wo die Zeit euch brennt."

The label "record" does indeed fit the mode of presentation employed in all six poems of the first thematic group (World War I; see p. 6) gathered in *Lebenslauf*. They all offer a scenic description of human action and experience, either by means of direct rendering of word and/or thought ("Die Hebamme spricht"; "Transportzug"), or by mediation through the filter of reminiscence ("Übers Feld, Mutter, ging ich dir weit entgegen"; "September"; "Augenblick aus dem Leben eines Kindes"), or by an imaginative *mise en scène* ("Kinder pflanzen einen Baum").

The title of the first poem, "Die Hebamme spricht" (LL 17–18; SL 11), identifies the chosen persona and her narrational role: "the midwife is speaking." In what follows, she quite literally gives a report of her professional routine and attendant observations and reflections: being woken up by the doorbell at night; being greeted, on arrival at the scene of the childbirth in progress, by the familiar sights, sounds, and smells of birth, life, and death in the crowded quarters of the poor; witnessing the cry of the new life already condemned. Making allowance for an unavoidable measure of stylization characteristic of the printed German word, the language put into the midwife's mouth comes close to natural speech and thus accords well with the "report" structure of the poem:

> Das ist immer das gleiche: ein fremdes Zimmer.
> Es riecht nach ungeborenem Leben, nach Schweiß,
> nach Angst, Noch-nicht-Gebären-Können und Urin.
> Und da ist eine Uhr und da ein Tisch,
> ein Teller mit Essen, Kopfkissen
> mit der Höhlung des nachtbedeckten Gesichts. (St. III)

Plainness of diction informs even the occasional figure of speech, for example, "wie das Leben der Frau den Becher hinhält" (st. i, line 3), or "wenn die Klingel den Traum zersplittert" (st. ii, line 1), or when the rudely awakened sleeper "den Schlaf schnell zurück-kämm[t]" (st. ii, line 3). The latter two images are notable examples of poetic expressiveness attained under the ethos of "Neue Sachlichkeit" which clearly guided the young poet's pen. The poem is most powerful where it speaks and describes in short, laconic sentences:

> Wie viele Zimmer hier sind – und alle so:
> Stockflecken an den Wänden, viele Betten
> oder was Betten gleichkommt, oben fällt der Putz. –
> In jedem: Geruch. In jedem: Menschen.
> Ich höre: das Haus atmet aus.
> Röhren, in denen es flüstert: der Abort. (St. v)

The picture of working-class squalor thus drawn is unforgettable; its emotive matter-of-factness foreshadows what will be one of the strong points of Bauer's mature poetry. This poem appears to be a worthy opening piece to his representative selection.

The poem "Transportzug" (LL 20; KS 85) "records" directly the thoughts and observations of a speaker implied by the plural pronoun "wir" and the related possessive adjective "unser" in the first line of the penultimate stanza (vi). The diction is carefully chosen, yet free of overt poetic stylization. The first stanza will serve as illustration:

> Die Soldaten im Feld haben nichts mehr, sie sind aller Dinge entäußert,
> sie tragen graue Uniformen, der Erde gleich, und Gewehr,
> sie fahren langsam täglich und in der Nacht daher,
> sie haben auch sich nicht mehr, bald geben sie sich dahin. (St. 1)

The poem does, however, possess an elaborate stanzaic organization. This is easily overlooked owing to the natural flow of its long lines. Of the seven stanzas, the first four are quatrains, followed by one couplet and two tercets. This asymmetrical sequence is held together by an overriding circular structure of thought and metric form. The opening quatrain (st. 1) speaks of the soldiers in the battlefield who, already stripped of everything, will soon be stripped of their lives as well. The following three quatrains (st. ii-iv) take the reader one chronological step back and describe how these sol-

diers are being transported, slowly but steadily, from life, via grow-
ing indifference, to death. The couplet that follows (st. v) restates
this process, trimming it down to its observable factual core: the
trains are passing through the station, leaving behind nothing but
the rapidly fading hum of the tracks which stay in place – "In der
Nacht fahren die Transportzüge durch die Station, / und die
Schienen bleiben zurück und bewahren noch eine Zeit den Ton"
(st. v) – for more trains to carry away more soldiers, as the reader
readily infers.

The first of the two tercets affords a glimpse of the embers of life
and desire that still glimmer behind the protective screen of indiffer-
ence. Passing houses where people actually get some sleep, they
would indeed like to interrupt their journey into death and enjoy
some sleep too:

Wenn sie unsre Häuser sehn, in denen wir schlafen,
möchten sie die tödliche Reise auch unterbrechen
und mit dem und jenen oder allein schlafen – (St. vi)

The second tercet, the last stanza of the poem, reverts immediately
to the given situation of disposable life and ongoing supply secured
from the younger generation who, too, "have already divested them-
selves of many things," as the last line states, and who will, accord-
ing to the poem's opening line, soon be "divested of all things":

Aber sie fahren vorüber, sie haben nichts mehr –
entfernen sich diese und sterben, fahren neue daher,
jüngere, auch diese haben sich schon vieler Dinge entäußert. (St. viii)

In similar manner, repetition of the phrase, "During the day they
sit" (st. ii, line 1) and "During the day they shout hurrah" (st. iii,
line 1; st. iv, line 1), serves to bring out the connection of the three
inner quatrains, and to identify each as a fresh attempt to focus on
these soldiers' death-bound journey from a different angle. Stanza ii
focuses on their changing estimation of the world they are leaving.
Many are finding out that they have loved the things in this world
more than they had realized:

Am Tag sitzen sie in den Wagen und schauen die Dinge an,
...
Mancher hat die Welt und dies und jenes in ihr mehr, als er wußte, geliebt.
                                                        (St. ii, lines 1; 4)

Stanza III brings into view their diminishing interaction with people. They still wave back to some children they are passing; at railway stations they may ask for something to eat or drink, or for nothing:

> und winken Kindern zu, die an den Schranken stehn und auch winken,
>
> ...
>
> mancher verlangt nichts, mancher auf den Stationen zu essen und trinken.
>
> (St. III, lines 2; 4)

Stanza IV, obviously the climax of this descriptive sequence, points up the contrast between the soldiers' day and night: while the former still affords a modicum of interaction with the surrounding world, the night will reveal the harsh truth of their situation and bring them, whatever they do, closer to their deaths:

> Am Tag schreien sie Hurra, und in der Nacht
> schlafen sie sich dem Tod zu, nur wer nicht schlafen kann
> im Geruch, sitzt auf dem Bagagewagen, raucht und wacht,
> wie das immer gleichgültig ist, sich auch dem Tod zu. (St. IV)

This point is underscored by yet another repetition of phrase: at night they "schlafen [...] sich dem Tod zu" (line 2), and those who cannot sleep sit outside and wake and smoke "sich auch dem Tod zu" (line 4). The climactic repetition in these two lines replaces their end rhyme, thereby varying emphatically the pattern of alternation shared by stanzas II (*c d c d*), III (*e f e f*) and IV (*g x g x*). End rhyme is again employed to define both the summarizing couplet that follows (st. V: *i i*) and the first of the two ensuing tercets (st. VI: *k x k*). The concluding tercet (st. VII) possesses a rhyme scheme (*b b a*) that agrees symmetrically with the first three lines of the opening quatrain (*a b b*), with rhyme *a* forming part of a phrase repetition already discussed. The following diagram will serve to illustrate the poem's structural composition:

st. I: 1...sie sind aller Dinge entäußert   *a*
     2...Gewehr   *b*
     3..daher   *b*
     4..........mehr.........................dahin   *x*

    st. II: 1.Am Tag sitzen sie in den Wagen ...   *c*
        2...   *d*
        3...   *c*
        4...   *d*

st. III: 1.Am Tag schreien sie Hurra............. *e*

    2 .... *f*

    3 .... *e*

    4 .... *f*

st. IV: 1.Am Tag schreien sie Hurra................................... *g*

    2.*schlafen sie sich dem Tod zu*.. *x*

    3 .... *g*

    4 ....*sich auch dem Tod zu* *x*

    st. V: 1.. *i*

          2.. *i*

    st. VI: 1... *k*

          2.möchten sie die tödliche Reise auch unterbrechen... *x*

          3.. *k*

st. VII: 1 .... *b*

    2 .... *b*

    3...........schon vieler Dinge entäußert *a*

A symmetrical frame of rhyme and repetition is built into this relatively long poem. Even the two lines that do not possess end rhyme (st. I, line 4; st. VI, line 2) appear to be faithfully worked into the pattern of the poem as a whole. The first of these two lines is integrated into the pattern of the stanza which it concludes (I) through an internal rhyme that echoes the end rhyme of the preceding two lines (2 and 3), and through the contrastive twin formula "daher" / "dahin" that connects it emphatically to the line that precedes immediately (3). In stanza VI, the absence of an integrating rhyme seems to underscore the thought expressed in line 2, namely, the idea that these doomed young men, as they pass the houses where normal sleep is still possible (line 1: *k*), would like to break away from their fateful journey (line 2: *x*) just to sleep like those fortunate enough not to be called to arms (line 3: *k*).

Is this over-interpretation? I do not think so. The poem strikes me as painstakingly composed, demonstrating the young poet's considerable skill in handling poetic form. While end rhyme, happily unobtrusive as one reads this poem, will not play a major role in Bauer's subsequent creative endeavour, contrast and repetition are two important devices that will be employed again and again to fashion a "Bericht" that speaks the language of art.

The observations related in "Transportzug" are taken straight from Bauer's childhood experience of World War I (see *GP* 82). They are, however, rendered as a third-person account whose distancing effect helps to transcend the purely personal by directing the reader's attention to the observed rather than the observer. The latter does bring himself in briefly and indirectly as part of the plural "we" and "our" in line 1 of stanza VI. The "we" / "they" opposition thus established brings into sharp focus the painful reality of the soldiers' journey into death.

Autobiographical material presented without such distancing is found in three of the six early poems here discussed. "September" (LL 22; KS 41) is a nostalgic reminiscence in which the speaker recalls imaginative childhood games rudely brought to an end by the exigencies of real life. This poem, too, is a "Bericht" in Bauer's sense: it is an account made interesting by its pattern of shifting perspectives. Starting out with a description of the remembered scene (In the Septembers of our childhood we lay in the fields roasting potatoes [lines 1–5]), the speaker, almost unnoticeably, slips into and shares the perspective of the children to whom the German potato field is a North American arena of Indian warfare (and talked about new expeditions because the Iroquois had come over the South Fork [lines 6–8]):

> In den Septembern der Kindheit
> waren Feuer auf den Feldern,
> und wir lagen ...
> ...
> und sprachen von neuen Kriegszügen,
> denn die Irokesen
> waren über den South Fork gekommen. (Lines 1–8)

This identification is broken by the interjection "O braunes kindliches Glück!" (line 9) which underscores the distance separating the happy then of childhood from the sober now of adult reality. The thread of reminiscence is resumed immediately, taking the speaker back again into the scene of playful fancy:

> War es nicht in den Septembern,
> daß wir
> unsere Kriegsbeile begruben. (Lines 10–12)

But then the hard facts of childhood impinged upon the child's capacity for imaginative play. The game was over because of the chief's poor school report; deprived of their leader, the children burned the boats of their imagination and went home:

denn unser Häuptling
hatte einen Zettel bekommen,
daß er nicht versetzt würde,
und wir hatten keinen Führer.
   O Trauer!
Und dann verbrannten wir
die hochbugigen schönen Schiffe
unserer Phantasie
…
und gingen heim. (Lines 15–24)

The exclamation, "O Trauer!" (line 19), graphically centred to catch the reader's attention, fuses adult nostalgia – possibly shot through with a measure of gentle irony – with the deep disappointment felt by the children torn away from their play. All this is narrated in the past tense, making the speaker's reminiscing perspective the dominant one.

The other two "autobiographical" poems also deal with childhood experience, but they do so in the straightforward manner of a first-person account. Because of its greater formal interest, only "Augenblick aus dem Leben eines Kindes" (*LL* 23; *KS* 27) will be considered here. Juxtaposition serves to bring together three separate but simultaneous war scenes, two at home and one at the front line: the then thirteen-year-old speaker lining up in front of a shop for some cold meat he was not to get (lines 1–6; 20–3); his grown-up brother concealing in his letter to his mother the actual state of affairs in the trenches just before following order to stagger to his almost desired death (lines 7–13); his mother crying in spite of her elder son's encouraging message, moved by her instinctual knowledge of his fate (lines 14–19). The speaker's own story provides the matrix into which the other two are inserted (my indentations):

Als ich am Nachmittag unter vielen Menschen stand
vor einem Laden, in dem es billige Wurst geben sollte,
(Lines 1–2)
    wünschte sich einmal mein Bruder im Feld fast:
    nicht mehr zu sein. Das war, als sie um diese Zeit
    in einem Graben lagen,…
    …
    … und die Toten rochen sehr –
    er schrieb es aber nicht, sondern schrieb nur:
    Liebe Mutter, mir geht es gut,
    (Lines 7–13)

aber meine Mutter weinte, als wüßte sie,
daß jetzt noch drei Minuten waren bis zum Sturm,
...
... bis der Leutnant seine Pfeife zog,
bis sie heraustaumelten und starben.
(Lines 14–19)
Das war, als ich dreizehnjährig unter Menschen stand
...
und ich brachte nichts heim als mich,
frierend and mit Hunger.
(Lines 20–3)

Bare, painful details strung together with almost Kleistian urgency and breathlessness – a powerful "Bericht" indeed.

The poem "Kinder pflanzen einen Baum" (LL 19; SL 13) borrows the immediacy of drama for much of its imaginative appeal. The speaker probably is a child who invites other children to participate in the planting of an apricot stone in anticipation of a tree that might yield fruit and put an end to their hunger. The dramatic nature of this piece is indicated by the introductory lines of the first two stanzas: "Kommt her, ihr Kinder, wir wollen etwas Feines machen" (st. I); "So, in das Loch legen wir ihn" (st. II). Intensifying the poem's appeal structure are the open-ended concluding lines of stanzas I and III, where dots issue an invitation to imagine the unspoken: "Wenn man solche Kerne in die Erde steckt, sagt sie, / werden Bäume daraus ..." (st. I, lines 4–5), "Alle würden satt ..." (st. III, line 6). The children are to imagine the marvel of a tree growing from a stone, and that of everyone having enough to eat, while the reader is invited to consider the innocent optimism of these children, their deprivation and, in spite of it, their desire to share. One clearly recognizes the hand of the humanist Walter Bauer.

To sum up the findings so far, the common denominator of the poems discussed in the preceding pages clearly is "Sachlichkeit." It identifies the young Bauer as a "comrade of his time" (a phrase he was to coin years later) and accords well with his notion of poetry as a "Bericht." It entails a tendency to use autobiographical material with little or no effort to veil this fact, and a plainness of diction which, while carefully chosen, does not intend to beautify and in that sense poeticize. Such natural speech seems most effective where it is reduced to short, laconic statement ("Die Hebamme spricht"). All poems give evidence of the young poet's close attention to the structuring of his material. This involves meticulous stanzaic organization based on rhyme, repetition, and contrast ("Transportzug"), shifting of perspectives ("September"), montage of simultaneous scenes

("Augenblick aus dem Leben eines Kindes") and imaginative drama-
tization ("Kinder pflanzen einen Baum").

> ⤲ *"Eure Worte sollen sein:*
> *Berichte aus der täglichen Schlacht.*
> *in die Gehirne einzuhämmern!"*

The second thematic group of poems included in Part One of *Lebens-
lauf* comprises seven pieces which give voice to the concerns that
arose in reaction to the various aspects and consequences of the
large-scale industrialization during and after World War I as Bauer
witnessed it in his native Thuringia. These poems attest to his strong
sense of solidarity with fellow human beings, a sense which tran-
scended national boundaries and embraced in particular the power-
less and patient victims of the dehumanizing forces unleashed by the
developments of the day.

These latter are the subject-matter of the short poem "Städte und
Werke" (LL 31; SL 95). Fourteen, mostly short, lines of factual, pithy
statement outline the environmental and human costs of the current
growth of cities and industrial plants: destruction of the earth as a
life–sustaining resource, growing isolation, loss of identity and vital-
ity, alienation from the earth. Written as one unit, the poem is clearly
divided into two seven-line sections. These are marked by two par-
allel statements anticipated in the title of the poem: "The cities are
growing" (line 1) and "The factories are growing" (line 8), each being
coupled with an even more emphatically parallel line that sums up
the price exacted by these developments: "Ever lonelier the human
being" (line 2) and "Ever higher the fences of sameness" (line 9). A
third anaphoric parallel is added to throw into sharp relief the con-
sequences for the future: "Soon one will have to travel far, / [to see
where there is green earth]" (lines 3–[4]), and: "Soon our faces will
be pits of night" (line 11):

Die Städte wachsen.
Immer einsamer wird der Mensch;
bald wird man weit reisen müssen (lines 1–3);

Die Werke wachsen.
Immer höher werden die Zäune des Gleichmaßes,
…
Bald werden unsre Gesichter Gruben der Nacht sein. (Lines 8–11)

The remaining three lines of the first section describe the present
process of environmental decay: the fields are drying and dying

under the ashes spewed out by the industrial plants: "The grain fields are getting thin, / ashes colour them brown, / and their fervour to blossom is dying" (lines 5–7). The remaining three lines of the second section predict the future result of human uniformity and alienation: "noone will recognize us, / the earth will have forgotten / who we are" (lines 12–14). Perfect parallelism of the two sections has been avoided by a variation in the placement of the anaphoric "bald – bald" (line 3 in the first section, line 4 in the second), and the reversal of the syntactic relationships: section 1: "bald wird man weit reisen müssen / zu sehn, wo grüne Erde ist" (lines 3–4); section 2: "Schornsteine dampfen ohne Hoffnung. / Bald werden unsre Gesichter Gruben der Nacht sein" (lines 3–4).

The connecting thread running through the parallel structure of this poem is spun by the verb "werden" which occurs in seven of the fourteen lines. The full verb with its meaning of "becoming" or "growing" is used three times (lines 2, 5, 9), the auxiliary verb forming part of the future tense, four times (lines 3, 11, 12, 13). Thus the poem's two principal concerns are emphatically delineated: present development and future consequence.

Contrasting sharply with the economy of "Städte and Werke" is the detailed expansiveness with which the poem "Meine gestorbenen Freunde" (LL 24–5; KS 94–6) expresses Bauer's sense of universal brotherhood and attendant personal responsibility. Again, the poem is carefully crafted, featuring parallelism, enumeration, and repetition-cum-variation as its major structuring devices.

Of the four parts that make up this poem, the first (stanza I) sets the scene: the speaker describes how, during quiet moments at night, he is visited by a sense of connection with other human hearts. These are remembered in the three stanzas (II-IV) of the second part. The bond of friendship by which the speaker feels united with these young victims of war is restated in the third part (stanza V). The fourth part (stanza VI) acknowledges moral responsibility accruing from their premature deaths, and expresses the speaker's resolution to fulfil it.

In stanza I, structural symmetry serves to focus on the moments of nightly meditation referred to in line 5: "nächtlich, wenn ich einen Augenblick vor dem Schlafengehen sitze." In such moments, the speaker recalls impulses received, but barely noticed, during his daily activities (lines 1–4). He now brings them to life imaginatively, hearing a "voice" within, feeling the touch of a "hand," sensing a "step" approaching him (lines 6–9). "Stimme" (line 7), "Hand" (line 8) and "Schritt" (line 9) provide the keywords for each of the three subsequent stanzas in which imagined "real" people are iden-

tified by name and place of birth and death. Parallelism and varia-
tion determine the structure of these three stanzas:

> Dies: ist die Stimme eines Menschen René Blanchard,
> geboren ...
> gelebt ...
> gefallen ...
> (St. ɪɪ)

> Dies: ist die Berührung auf meinem Scheitel der Hand
> eines Menschen George Andrews,
> geboren ...
> gefallen ...
> (St. ɪɪɪ)

> Das: ist der leise Schritt eines siebzehnjährigen Menschen
> Kolja Stenkin,
> geboren ...
> erfroren ...
> (St. ɪv)

Stanza v sets in with another repetition of phrase, employed to
throw into relief the speaker's guilt and shame vis-à-vis his "friends"
whose death he failed to ease or prevent:

> Das sind, die meine Freunde werden sollten,
> das sind, die meine Freunde waren und gestorben sind,
> weil ich zu schwach war, aufzustehn, sie zu stützen im Fallen.
> (St. v, lines 1–3)

Once again, the names of the three "gefallenen Freunde in der Welt"
are invoked (line 4), followed by two images reaffirming the
speaker's keen sense of connection with them (lines 5–6).

The final stanza, the longest in the poem (12 lines), falls into two
parts. The first speaks of the young dead soldiers' un-lived joys and
sorrows now to be "filled" by the more fortunate survivor (lines 1–7).
Three kinds of "Freuden," appropriate to the homelands of the dead,
are itemized – sailing in the harbour at Cherbourg, hunting bears in
the forests of Canada, celebrating Easter in Russia:

> die Segelfreuden in den Hafenwassern von Cherbourg [René],
> die Jagd auf den Bär in den kanadischen Wäldern [George],
> die Osterfeier am vollen, brechenden Tisch [Kolja]. (St. vɪ, lines 3–5)

In contrast, "sorrows and disappointments" (line 6) remain unexemplified – a welcome release from the barrage of meticulously structured detail. However, no word is spared to spell out the "moral" emerging from all this – to speak, to love, to remember:

> und ich habe mir vorgenommen,
> in der Müdigkeit der Trambahn und im Lesen der Journale in den Lesehallen,
> zu sprechen und zu lieben alle, die zu lieben ihr nicht Zeit hattet,
> die Erde zu lieben und der Gabe zu denken,
> die ihr mir gebracht habt schweigend im stummen Gehorsam.
>
> (St. VI, lines 8–12)

Line 9 returns to the speaker's daily activities already referred to at the beginning of the poem (st. I, lines 3–4), thus closing the frame around a heavily laden verbal artifact whose structured finesse verges on pedantry, whose emotional charge seems hard to bear.

Heavy emotion, also, informs the shorter piece, "Unfaßbare Stunde" (LL 32; SL 68), which renders a similar moment of meditative communion with the world. However, emotion, rather than being poured out in front of the reader, is called up largely to activate the reader's affective response. The title of the poem, repeated and enlarged upon in the opening line of the concluding section (st. II, line 1), points up the "incomprehensible" and deeply moving fact that human beings can, provided they have the appropriate attitude and necessary technology, communicate with each other across great distances. A human being, sitting in front of a radio, is waiting – all ear, all heart – for good news:

> O Welt! Unfaßbare Stunde –
> sieh hier:
> ein Mensch ist aufgespannt wie der Empfänger,
> ganz Ohr, ganz Herz,
> und wartet auf gute Nachricht aus dem Unendlichen.
> Und eine Stimme sagt ganz klar, langsam:
> Moskau – (St. II)

The religious overtones borrowed here are obvious, thanks to an implied reversal of the well-worn "oh world"-plaint (line 1); a touch of biblical diction: "behold" (line 2); a variation on the theme of glad tidings from heaven: "waiting for good news from infinity" (line 5). The emotive force of such borrowing is cunningly enhanced in light of the rejection of religion with which the poem begins. No prayer for us, no fear of church or heaven:

> Wir rufen nicht an,
> gefaltete Hände, was soll das?
> Die Angst vor schwarzem Talar, vor dem Himmel –
> vorbei – (St. 1, lines 1–4)

In pronouncing a ban on religion while at the same time using it as a source of evocative material, the poet has found a clever way of lending weight to his this-wordly stance. Its communist orientation is clearly indicated by the name "*Moskau*," italicized and mentioned twice (st. 1, line 12; st. 11, line 7). It is from here, not from "heaven" (st. 1, line 3), that the religiously waited-for voice speaks clearly and slowly (st. 11, line 6). Its message, however, remains unspoken and the reader is given free rein to draw his or her own conclusions. This poem, then, written in 1930, while not entirely free of potentially jarring emotion ("und das Zimmer ist erfüllt / von der hohen Rührung des Unfaßbaren, Einsamen" [st. 1, lines 15–16]), is cogent evidence of the young Bauer's growing mastery of his metier.

"Tödlicher Unglücksfall auf Bau 43" (*LL* 29; *KS* 55) is designed to involve its reader in a similar manner, addressing both his/her imaginative and cognitive faculties. The poem retraces a rust remover's last hours before his fatal "accident," caused in an instant of recognition by a vision of life away from the rusty monotony of his own. The story is told in nine stanzaic units of free verse. The crucial moment is thrown into relief rhetorically by two parallel lines highlighting the man's sudden sense of estrangement and complete dissociation from his depressing world: "Da dachte er wie einer, der hier völlig fremd ist" (st. vii, line 1); "Da dachte er wie einer, der völlig fertig ist hier" (st. viii, line 1). In the lines that follow these two signposts, repetition, variation, and contrast join forces to suggest, in a few powerful strokes, the mental processes that caused him to "fall": a vision of a beautiful seascape, of free movement in the wind and along the horizon, of a lovely house he might live in – contrasting sharply with the actual sight of thirteen chimneys surrounding him like a fence, and of the rusty wall he had to scrape at a prescribed rate per hour:

> an ein Seebild, und wie schön war
> eine Fahne im Winde, und ein Pferd
> ging braun über den Horizont. (St. vii, lines 2–4)

und sah die dreizehn Schornsteine wie einen Zaun,
wie schön das Haus wäre, in dem er wohnte,
und die Wand, von der er Rost abkratzen sollte,
drei Quadratmeter die Stunde – und fiel. (St. VIII, lines 2–5)

Without being exposed to a lot of detail, the reader knows and understands exactly what went on. The final point of the poem, this individual's expendability, is reported in like matter-of-factness of word and tone:

und niemand von den Hingeeilten wußte, wie
er hinging ohne Trauer, Buße, Wort, nur
daß er wegging, schnell, daß
seine Invalidenkarte ungültig wurde,
und ein andrer, der Rost abkratzte, war. (St. IX, lines 5–9)

Bauer's penchant for narration does indeed seem to produce the best results when he confines himself to plain statement without elaborate rhetoric or comment. The poem "Arbeiter zieht ein reines Hemd an" (LL 28; SL 109) is a splendid example. It describes a worker returning home from work, washing, putting on a clean shirt, sitting down to eat and enjoying, with barely a word, the preciousness of just being ("die schönste Gegenwart," st. V, line 2). This is narrated in laconic "Zeilenstil" with only one enjambement occurring half-way through the poem (st. III, lines 3–4) where the narrator allows himself a pointed aside: "One might believe that so much tough grime / won't come off completely even with the sharpest of soap":

Er zieht das Hemd aus, das ganz schwarz geworden ist,
er wäscht sich ganz, weil das am Sonnabend so Sitte ist.
Man könnte glauben, soviel zäher Dreck
geht auch mit scharfer Seife nicht mehr gänzlich weg,
sitzt schwer im Herzen fest. (St. III)

The predominant pattern of minimal statement of action, accompanied only by a necessary complement or explanation, effectively renders the repetitive, unquestioning simplicity of this worker's Saturday-night bliss: "Er fährt mit einem kleinen Licht am Rad nach Haus" (st. I, line 1); "Er tritt zur Stube ein, als käm er aus der Nacht" (st. II, line 1); "Er zieht das Hemd aus, das ganz schwarz geworden ist" (st. III, line 1); "Er fühlt den Stoff an seinem Leib, er ist ganz rein" (st. IV, line 4); "Er spricht mit seiner Frau nicht viel, weil er jetzt langsam ißt" (st. v, line 3). End rhyme is employed in fairly regular pattern (*a a b b x* in the 5-line stanzas: I, III, IV, V; *a a x x* in stanza II) to hammer home the impression of unrelieved and unreflected monotony.

Where explicit judgment is added, Bauer draws on the tried and trusted form of the ballad which traditionally allowed such an ending. "Ballade vom jungen erschossenen Arbeiter" (*LL* 33–4; *SL* 83–4) tells the story of a young (probably communist) worker being released from detention in a silo, and shot as if in flight. The narrator's concluding comment repeats, as a stanzaic unit and with important variation of wording and punctuation, a three-line section of the first stanza centring on the saying, "Ehre wem Ehre gebührt." What the young man deserved but did not receive (st. I) must be refused to murderers (st. VII). A subtle shift in the meaning of the word "Gemeine" (from "common soldiers" in st. I, to "mean persons" in st. VII) adds to the force of the accusation:

sie waren drei, ein Unteroffizier und zwei Gemeine,
Ehre, wem Ehre gebührt,
ihm aber erwiesen sie keine (emphasis added). (St. I, lines 3–5)

Es waren drei, ein Unteroffizier und zwei Gemeine.
Ehre wem Ehre gebührt.
Mördern gebührt keine (emphasis added). (St. VII)

Thus the typically closed form of the ballad serves to round off the account of this horrifying occurrence with duly emphatic moral condemnation; it serves also to ward off any objection by a modern reader who may not care for this kind of moralizing.

Imagery – not one of Bauer's priorities, and so far considered only incidentally – is put to effective use in the poem "Streik" (*LL* 26–7; *SL* 103). Metonymic transfer of human qualities to the buildings and machines of the industrial plant where the strike is staged pervades five of the poem's six sections. A few examples will suffice: "Der Bagger kann die Erde nicht mehr fressen" (st. I, line 3); "Der Herzschlag der Schweißapparate in den Kesseln ist verstummt" (st. II, line 3); "der Wind wartet auf die Wolke der Schornsteine (st. III, line 5); "erstarrt ist die Faust des Krans" (st. IV, line 6); "die Bahnhöfe schweigen" (st. V, line 2). Such personification suggests active solidarity on the part of the buildings, machines, and even the elements, making all the more powerful the threat issued to the plant's management. Underscoring this point is the fright experienced by the security guard who has not joined the strikers: "Und abends, wenn der Wächter durch die Säle geht / im Schein des Lichts, erschrickt er tief –" (st. IV, lines 1–2).

Preparing, by way of summary, the point of the whole description – *"We, however, know what we are doing!"* (st. VI, line 5; italics in the original) – the final stanza uses an entirely new set of images. A stone has been thrown into "the sea of activity," disrupting it with sudden force and creating waves of expanding rings on the surface of the water. This image is to render the sudden disruption caused by the strike, and the ensuing expansion of the strike movement:

> In das Meer der Tätigkeit
> ist ein Stein geworfen worden,
> die Kreise wachsen. (St. VI, lines 1–3)

The final image describes this movement as a universal withdrawal and gathering in preparation of the final "defence": "die ganze Welt zieht sich zusammen zu Abwehr" (st. VI, line 4). All of this, the concluding line asserts provocatively, is an entirely rational and therefore justified course of action: *"Wir aber wissen, was wir tun!"*

In sum, the second group of poems adds to the variety of the young Bauer's "Bericht"-poetry. Meticulous structuring continues to prevail, with parallelism, repetition, and variation serving as principal agents of order and emphasis. Their effectiveness tends to rise or fall with the degree of restraint ("Städte und Werke"; "Unfaßbare Stunde") or expansiveness ("Meine gestorbenen Freunde") of description and expression. Suggestion ("Tödlicher Unglücksfall auf Bau 43") and laconism ("Arbeiter zieht ein reines Hemd an") are found beside exploitation of imagery ("Streik") and poetic genre ("Ballade vom jungen erschossenen Arbeiter").

At the beginning of Bauer's poetic career, then, stand the narrative poem with its virtually unlimited freedom, and the formal challenge this freedom entails. The young poet clearly worked hard to meet this challenge, making use of an impressive variety of forms and devices drawn mainly from the vast storehouse of traditional rhetoric.

Critical Strategies

~{ *"Richtig war zu meiner Zeit,*
Scharfsichtig zu sein, wachsam, verschlossen."

The poems written during the National Socialist era and during World War II offer an illuminating "record" of Bauer's observations, thoughts, and feelings during those years. While the selections included in *Lebenslauf* reflect more accurately the later Bauer's preference and judgment, they still give a good idea both of his preoccupations and creative tendencies at the time.

Of the thirteen pieces that found their way into *Lebenslauf*, four give evidence of some camouflage strategies the poet appears to have adopted in an attempt to slip his poetry past the censors' desk into print. Another eight poems form a homogeneous group of "messages from beyond," voicing openly Bauer's deep sense of disgust, horror, and guilt about the ravages of war and racism. Heading this entire group is the expansive poem "Der neue Krieg" (35–6), sole survivor of the manuscript "Menschenstimme" of 1933 that fell victim to the flames of censorship (*LL* 8). Bauer included it in his representative selection in order to document his early anticipation of the events that were to unfold after that fateful year. He was wise enough to disclaim "first-rate" quality for this image-laden and heavy piece of rhetoric which predicts Germany's demise as a result of "Europe's last war" (line 9).

What this poem has in common with most of the other pieces in the group is an "outsider" perspective of superior insight. In this case, the speaking "I," who reports and comments on the apocalyptic occurrences of this ultimate burst of destruction, places himself clearly above those, addressed as "ihr," who were misguided by false ideas: "Da liegt ihr! / Dachtet ihr nicht weiterzukommen?" is the censorious preamble to his concluding sally: "Da liegt Deutschland. / Da lag Deutschland."

The outsider *par excellence* is portrayed by the two companion pieces, "Bildnis eines Astronomen" (LL 37; GE 46) and "Bildnis eines Geologen" (LL 38; GE 47). On the face of it, these two scientists lack interest in the people around them (the geologist) or even avoid them deliberately (the astronomer), prompted by their own paramount professional preoccupation. However, the astronomer's portrait indicates clearly that he has turned his back on humanity because it is a faceless, passion-driven collection of thieves:

> Die Universumgesichter der Sterne sind ihm bekannter als die Larven der
>   Erdballbewohner, von Leidenschaft verzerrt. (St. I, line 4)

> Seine Gärten liegen auf dem Sirius, vor Dieben geschützt. (St. II, line 2)

One may safely assume that the target of Bauer's criticism here is the inhumanity of his time. Couched in universal terms, his real criticism was effectively veiled to those of lesser literary sensitivity. Those who could see through the veil would easily understand that this poem is in effect talking about the alienated contemporary poet who tends "his gardens" on a distant star, away from human beings, in order to give the peace he is planting a chance to grow:

> Seine Gärten liegen auf dem Sirius, vor Dieben geschützt,
> ...
> und [er] pflanzt, der hier so schlecht gedeihen will,
> ewigen Frieden auf jenem kleinen Sterne ein,
> da er dort keine Menschen vermutet. (St. II, lines 2; 6–8)

The garden metaphor, as old as poetry itself, provides the key. Needless to explain who the "thieves" are in this scheme of things. Ironically, the poet does what he does for the benefit of those from whom he flees: "Aber für sie sucht er den Raum nach Geheimnissen ab" st. I, line 7). Here is Bauer's own situation in a nutshell: "inner" and later also "outer" emigration spent in untiring work to find and cultivate the word of humanism for those who could not or would not hear him.

The veil of indirection is drawn more tightly around the geologist's portrait. However, read in conjunction with the astronomer's portrait, it readily yields access to its hidden dimension. While the astronomer's familiarity with the "faces of the stars" (st. I, line 4) points to the superior insights attained by the poet's soaring mind and spirit, the geologist has dominion over the vast reaches of earth's depths, temporal and spatial:

Er ist der Herr aller Schätze, Herr verstorbener Mammutherden, versun-
kener Erdteile, des Neandertales sorgsamer Vater.
Er könnte trinken aus den Quellen aller Amazonenströme.
Furchtlos bewegt er sich unter der Last von Ozeanen. (St. I, lines 3–5)

This suggests the poet's far-reaching and thorough grasp of the
essence of things, their dimensions, their roots, their core – to the
extent of being able to reach a state of *unio mystica*, "deadly" to
others, a "triumph" to himself:

Ah! Sein Triumph:
zu sinken unter alle Meere durch wachsende Glut –
die Erde: weich, ein Brei, tödlich für alle Hungrigen.
Meer flüssigen Gesteins, das All ein Feuerstrom!
Und aufzusteigen dann nach ungeheurem Fall! (St. II, lines 4–8)

And while the "astronomer" part of the poet escapes to the remotest
corner of the universe to plant goodness there, the "geologist" part
has to delve deep down to the centre of the earth to find it: "Sein
Auge nimmt allmählich den Glanz des Erdkerns an / und wird gren-
zenlos gütig" (st. III, lines 7–8).
    However, he is unable to share his precious find with the people
around him; they would not understand:

Wenn er in der Straßenbahn fährt, merkt niemand, daß seine Hand sorglos
mit unentdeckten Metallen spielt.
Er könnte Blumensträuße aus dem Karbon verschenken. (St. III, lines 4–5)

The subjunctive is significant: "He *could* give them bouquets from
the Carboniferous period" (line 7), but he is wise enough not to. The
criticism here voiced remains veiled almost to the point of being
hidden. Such obliqueness is rare in Bauer's poetry. His fundamental
desire for clarity of statement appears to have been overruled by
strategic considerations prompted by the political situation of the
day.
    Another route he followed during those difficult years was the
path of old-fashioned poetic beauty. The volumes *Tagebuchblätter aus
Frankreich* (published in 1941) and *Gast auf Erden* (1943) contain a
number of poems composed in regular metre, ordered by regular
rhyme, often infused with a heavy dose of sentiment. It is a measure
of the later Bauer's good judgment that he included only two sam-
ples in his important *Lebenslauf*, apparently unswayed by the enor-
mous popularity which his *Tagebuchblätter* had enjoyed at the time of

their publication. They were hailed as "eine köstliche Meditation des deutschen Herzens mit der Hand am Gewehr" (cited by Riedel, *Wanderer* 177). The poems gathered in this volume are quite unreadable today.

"Der Frieden" (LL 40; TF 17), for example, is shot through with problematic poeticism. Bauer's familiar long lines are gathered into four couplets in which a traveller (a soldier in a "Transportzug"?) tells of a peaceful scene he once passed that reminded him of a pastoral idyll painted by Mellet, complete with shepherdess and sheep, a delicately coloured sky, grass and clover:

> Im Vorüberfahren sah ich's wie auf einem Bilde von Mellet:
> unterm zarten Himmel saß ein Schäfermädchen still in Gras
> und Klee. (St. i)

> Um sie lagen ihre Schafe, tiefer Daseinsruh ergeben,
> und das Mädchen hob die Gerte traumhaft, so, als wollte sie
> der Erde sanfte Schläge geben. (St. ii)

He decided to interpret it as an image of much hoped-for peace: "War dies Frieden? Oh, so war es, anders wollt' ich's mir nicht deuten" (st. iii, line 1). As this picture receded from sight, another one emerged, bringing into view a helmet on a grave, almost grown over by the summer grass: "Stumm versank das Bild des Mädchens und ein anderes stieg empor: / schweigend sah ich einen Helm auf einem Grabe, das sich fast im Sommergras verlor" (St. iv). A contrast seems intended here, one to bring out the heart-rending reality of war that lies behind the intense yearning for peace to which he earlier gave voice. At the same time, a reassuring message is conveyed: once the war is over the wounds will heal. However, the gentle tone of the entire poem, its rhythmic flow, its predictable rhyme echoes, and particularly the sweetness of its concluding summer-grass image seem disturbingly out of tune with the horror signalled by the helmet on the grave.

As Walter Riedel explains, Bauer's *Tagebuchblätter aus Frankreich* were conceived by Bauer as a personal affirmation of European thought and sensibility, and they were seized upon by his readers as a peaceful oasis in the midst of war and dying (*Wanderer* 188). The heritage of German romanticism is evident, particularly in the idea of death hailed as a gateway to a new mode of being and becoming. Evident also are oversentimentality and bathos:

> Ich presse mich im Feuer auf die Erde,
> bis ins Geheimnis ihres Wesens fühl ich sie.

Vom Tod umringt, spür' ich im Tod das Werde –
ich fühl' mich frei wie nie.

Ich höre deinen Schritt, o Tod, mir näher klingen,
mit glühenden Fäusten schlägst du auf mich ein.
Ich fühle dich wie Feuer in mich dringen –
o sag: zum Nichts? Zu neuem Sein? ("Verse eines Soldaten,"

TF 10, st. III-IV)

The poem "Bei einem Abschied" (LL 39; GE 91) renders what must
be a soldier's farewell from a loved one. This is done in such general
and sentimental terms that the situation seems unbearably trivial-
ized. The last stanza (V) will suffice:

Was du mir gegeben, halt ich,
bis es tagt.
Lebe wohl, nun wieder
wird die Fahrt gewagt.

The poems discussed so far in this chapter undertake, in varying
manner and degree, to veil, to mollify, or even to spiritualize. The
next group to be considered, taken from unpublished manuscripts
titled "Botschaften" (1944–46), consists of poems that abandon poetic
beauty and indirection and spell out what they have to say explicitly
and emphatically. The familiar "I"-account is used throughout, but
autobiographical connotations have been erased almost completely.
The speaker in every poem is the ultimate outsider: a dead person
– victim of the "new war" (including the Holocaust) which Bauer
had predicted a decade earlier. Thus the immediacy of a first–person
account and the authoritative distance of the chosen persona are
made to work hand in hand. Long lines and free verse have been
reinstated, excesses of structuring rhetoric largely avoided. In all
eight poems, the speaker possesses superior knowledge and there-
fore addresses the living as a teacher and admonisher. The penulti-
mate line of the first poem explains: "Tote haben die Einsicht
gefunden, die ihnen das Leben versagte" (LL 42: line 4). The "mes-
sages" they send to those still walking on the earth are varied: crit-
icism, exhortation, encouragement, regret, condemnation – all
joining forces to convey Bauer's appeal: shake off the fetters of rou-
tine and complacency, live with, and learn from, the past to create a
humane world.

These poems illustrate clearly Bauer's favoured practice of cumu-
lative variation. A certain concern is expressed repeatedly, varying
angles of approach serving to throw light on diverse aspects of the

matter. The pivotal point of such variation is the speaker's identity. In the poem "Sinken Engel schneller zur Erde..." (*LL* 41–2) he is a *Luftwaffe*-pilot who went down over Crete and is now buried there together with other nationals. He urges that those still living and engaged in the making of peace be told to act as if they possessed the wisdom of the dead: "Sag ihnen, sie wollen den Frieden so schaffen, / Als säßen die Toten an ihren Tischen" (lines 27–8).

Remaining unidentified in three other poems, the speaker has some very unpalatable things to say about the living and their incorrigible ways. In the poem "Wenn ich zurückgekommen wäre –" *LL* 43) he ponders the fact that in spite of experiences that should move people to mend their ways, they will not do so:

Du sagst, sie reden, reden und tun das Gleiche?
Immer das Gleiche wie einst?
...
Du sagst, sie feilschen um Stellen, ersticken in Wasserfällen von Worten?
(Lines 15–16; 20)

They will talk and act the way they have always done – and drown in their words. He therefore resigns himself to the silence of his own death, asking not to be mentioned to "these fools" as he would rather "sleep": "O diese Narren – meine Brüder. / Sag ihnen nichts von mir. Ich will schlafen" (lines 21–2).

In the poem "Ich bin schon fast unkenntlich" (*LL* 44), the dead admonitor laments people's innate forgetfulness. Those who survived will always return to their lives; for a while they will speak of the times they endured and, getting on with their lives, they will forget:

Immer gingen die Lebenden in ihr Leben zurück
und sprachen von mehr oder weniger großer Zeit.
...
Dann kommt das Gras.
...
Das Wehen des Grases klingt wie: Vergessen, vergessen.
Wie Spott. (Lines 12–13; 17; 21–2)

This is his scathing verdict: "Ich glaube, es ist besser, alle rotten sich aus. / Der Mensch ist die Erde nicht wert" (lines 23–4).

To counterbalance such harsh words, the poem "Ihr seid blind und stumpf geworden" (*LL* 48) gives voice to the hope he still harbours for them, blind and insensitive as they may be, encouraged by his first-hand experience of earth's continued life:

Ich möchte aufspringen und alle Gräber auftürmen zum Berg,
Euch in die stumpfen Ohren schreien:
Die Erde lebt! Hoffnung für euch! (Lines 19–21)

The speaker is also a young poet killed in action well before his genius had matured to give the world the joy it so urgently needs ("An der Straße von Treviso nach Castelfranco," LL 45). He is an actor who, having played death on the stage often and well, is now acquainted with the reality of death: unimaginable, unplayable ("An einem Abend war ich König," LL 46–7). He is a Holocaust victim appealing, without forgiveness, to the conscience of those who knew but did nothing to stop the "Ausverkauf des Menschen" – ("Sprich, wenn du zurückkommst –" LL 49). He is, finally, Everyman ("Jedermanns Botschaft," LL 51–2), articulating Bauer's principal message to everyone – "create a humane earth":

Schafft eine menschliche Erde dem Menschen.
…
Das ist dann Jedermanns Sieg. Vielleicht,
Vielleicht wird Gott dann noch einmal das Werk der Schöpfung beginnen,
Das wir verrieten … (Lines 11; 21–3)

As we noted earlier, the humanist Bauer does not hesitate to exploit religious allusion to intensify his plea. He concludes this poem with a biblical reference that will be understood by Everyman:

Licht war das erste Wort.
Nacht – o hört Jedermanns Botschaft –
Wird Nacht unser letztes Wort sein? (Lines 32–4)

The poetry written during the National Socialist era shows Bauer devising ways to meet the new challenges posed by the "documentary," essentially critical poem he chose to write. One method was that of withdrawal into aestheticizing traditionalism ("Verse eines Soldaten") or universality ("Bei einem Abschied"; "Frieden"), entailing the danger of burying his deep concerns under a veneer of triviality. Another, more successful method rested on the invention of an outsider's perspective to serve as a vehicle of veiled criticism ("Bildnis eines Astronomen"; "Bildnis eines Geologen"). The "outsider" poems whose critical voice speaks directly ("Botschaften") were not submitted for publication. Written immediately before and after the end of the war, these poems anticipate clearly Bauer's critical evaluation of postwar West German society.

⇥ *"Aber die Wüste wächst."*

Just as the selection of poems written during Germany's dark decade was prefaced by an emotionally intense long poem predicting the collapse that would mark the end of all, so the selection of postwar poetry is prefaced by an equally intense and expansive piece, giving voice to the poet's hope for a new beginning, envisioned as a rebirth of Europe in the hearts of her son(s). Written in May 1945, the poem "Ich bin dein Sohn, Europa" (LL 53–7; DT 38–42) is a straight piece of autobiographical documentation, saturated with Bauer's own sincerity of feeling and intention. It is almost entirely free of imagery and figuration and thus presents the purest "record" so far of what this one person "perceived, thought and felt." Important in the context of this enquiry is a recognition of two things: first, the broad sweep with which Bauer gathers childhood memory and wartime experience in order to integrate them, well ordered, in the present pulsation of a visionary rebirth; secondly, the detail and explicitness with which thoughts and feelings are being recorded both phenomenally and *in actu*. This is how the poem ends:

> Ah, Fülle der Gesichte, zuviel, um alles zu sagen, zuviel für mein Herz.
> …
> Unzählige Geburtsstätten hast du in diesen Tagen, in denen die Nacht mit
>   dem Morgenlicht kämpft.
> Sieh auch mich an, hier, in meinem kleinen Zelt, nahe der Erde, die wir
>   so lange gepeinigt.
> Ich trage dich in mir. Auch in mir wirst du von neuem geboren.
> Nein: ich verlor dich ja nie.
> Ich trage dich in mir. Ich bin dein Sohn, heimgekommen zu dir.
> Auch ich bin Europa. (St. IX, lines 1; 7–12)

Overwhelmed by visions too numerous to express, the speaker declares his unbroken commitment to the earth that has been tortured too long; his heart, like countless others, will serve as a cradle of her new birth; he, too, *is* Europe.

Detail, sensitively selected, is found in the short poem "Morgens" (LL 59; DT 87), which Bauer decided to place almost immediately after his paean to Europe, thus providing a welcome change from confessional prolixity to lyrical economy. The image of the "dawn of the world" entering the room "on golden feet" (st. 1) may not be very original, but the observed details gathered in the following two stanzas are richly suggestive:

> Sie fragt nicht,
> wem der Tisch gehört, an dem wir sitzen.
> Mit frischem Golde deckt sie seine Narben.

Sie fragt nicht: ist das euer Bett,
in dem die Nacht den Schlaf verschenkte.
Sie taucht die grauen Tücher
in einen Strom von Licht.
Und die geborstenen Tassen füllt sie
bis zum Rande
mit der Freude des jungen Tags. (St. II-III)

The scars of the table (st. II, line 3), the grey linen (st. III, line 3), the cracked cups (st. III, line 5) evoke powerfully the dilapidation and the poverty in which one lived immediately after the end of the war. The questionable means of survival to which people were reduced in those days are effectively inscribed into this slender text through the implication of unlawful possession of table and bed: "She [the dawn] doesn't ask / at whose table we are sitting" (st. II, lines 1–2); "she doesn't ask: is it your bed in which night granted sleep" (st. III, lines 1–2). The image of sleep being received as a gift from night points subtly but clearly to the pain, physical and mental, suffered as a result of the prevailing conditions. Against the backdrop of all this, the joy the young day brings with it is immensely enhanced.

The optimism expressed by this poem soon gave way to growing disappointment, accompanied by an increasingly critical stance, which less than a decade later moved Bauer to put an ocean between himself and the part of the world to which he felt so closely connected. The growth of this critical distance has been concisely "recorded" by the nine poems that conclude the European part of Bauer's *Lebenslauf*.

One may easily overlook the critical dimension of the first of these mostly short pieces, for example "Notiz" (*LL* 58; *OH* 13). The speaker pauses to ponder what, in the hour of Germany's new beginning, is now hailed by all newspapers as "new":

Das Neue, wovon sie reden
auf allen Seiten ihrer Zeitungen,
was ist es doch? Wo fand ich es?
Ist es so neu? (Lines 1–4)

He remembers incidents from recent experience which seem to indicate that the spirit of friendly cooperation, apparently now embraced as the "new" ethos, was alive, albeit in fragmentary fashion, during the times of hostility and war: an Italian woman had refreshed him, a German soldier, with a glass of water; an old Jew had acknowledged with silent astonishment a friendly gesture extended to him

by the same shamefaced German; a total stranger, hidden from view
by the darkness of night, had wished him good luck:

> Eine italienische Frau, in den Kämpfen des Rückzugs,
> gab mir ein Glas Wasser.
> Ein alter Jude, den ich zuerst in die Straßenbahn einsteigen ließ,
>   weil ich mich plötzlich schämte,
> sah mich erstaunt an.
> Eine fremde Stimme sprach mit mir und wünschte mir Glück,
> als unsere Züge nachts nebeneinander standen – (Lines 7–12)

The poem seems to be an affirmation of man's capacity for consid-
eration and kindness in times both of peace and of adversity. How-
ever, the scornful turn of the phrase "What they are talking about on
all pages of their newspapers" (lines 1–2) signals the speaker's dis-
approval of the new media rhetoric that contrasts sharply with the
quietness of the true friendliness he has experienced in real life both
inside and outside Germany.

Elusive in much the same way is the contemporary criticism incap-
sulated in the ambiguity of the relatively long piece "Zu meiner
Zeit" (LL 61–2; OH 61–2). This poem speaks of a society thrown into
chaos and terror by the use and abuse of words (lines 1–24); a short
excerpt will suffice:

> Zu meiner Zeit
> hatten viele Worte verschiedene Bedeutungen,
> je nach Land und Anschauung, je nach der Partei.
> ...
> Der Turm von Babel war ein Scherz
> den Mißverständnissen meiner Zeit gegenüber... (Lines 1–3; 8–9)

It speaks of survival depending on clear–sightedness, vigilance, and
reserve: "Richtig und meiner Zeit entsprechend war es, / sich auf
das eine oder andere gefaßt zu machen" (lines 25–6). "Richtig war
zu meiner Zeit, / scharfsichtig zu sein, wachsam, verschlossen"
(lines 38–9). The poem speaks of the need to work patiently towards
a cleansing of language:

> Gut war es aber trotz allem –
> geduldig daran zu arbeiten,
> daß die Worte wieder rein wurden
> und das Licht des Anfangs wieder erhielten. (Lines 30–3)

It urges one never to lose the ability to laugh – laughter probably
being the last remnant of our otherwise lost divine origin:

denn Lachen war, vielleicht, noch der einzige Sieg
über die Finsternis
und der letzte Rest
elend vertanen oder verlorengegangenen
göttlichen Ursprungs. (Lines 43–7)

All this is set in the past, suggesting that "my time" refers to the years of National Socialist abuse and terror. A long list of "real words" ("die wirklichen Worte," line 14) serves to substantiate this reading. The most obvious of them are "spying, passport confiscation, safe custody, arrest ... concentration camp, deportation for voluntary labour service ... liquidation": "Bespitzelung, Paßentzug, Sicherheitsverwahrung, Haft, ... Konzentrationslager, Zwangsverschickung zu freiwilligem Arbeitsdienst ... Liquidierung" (lines 17–21). However, may not "my time" also be the time when the poem was written (published in 1953), but referred to in the past tense from an imaginatively anticipated future point of view, when the Germany before and the Germany after the war will be seen as having been essentially the same?

The presence of such a sub-text is borne out by the criticism of contemporary life voiced in poems placed in *Lebenslauf* before and after "Zu meiner Zeit." The poem "Einem Fremden etwas zeigend" (*LL* 65; *OH* 52), takes a stranger on a guided tour through a town ravaged by the flames of war. The guide (and speaker of the poem), in a tone of friendly but relentless matter-of-factness, describes scenes of devastation haunting the memory of the town. He dwells at length on the cellars, "Orte des Wartens auf Tod oder Verschontwerden" (line 15):

Und dann: in diesen Kellern – sehen Sie? –
aus denen Unkraut hervorweht und kalter Totengeruch zerfetzter Zeit –
in diesen Kellern wartete man.
Auf was? möchten Sie wissen ... – Daß man übrigblieb. (Lines 10–13)

It was in these cellars that people spent "endlos scheinende Lehrstunden für eine andere Welt" (line 20). The "other world" is clearly ambiguous, referring both to the world beyond death and the world after the war. While the visitor's implied query whether these lessons were learned brings into focus the world after the war, the guide's "answer," a literal repetition of the question – "Ob die Prüfung bestanden wurde, fragen Sie?" (line 21) – suggests strongly that the real answer cannot be "yes."

The lesson not learned is the subject of two poems in this group. "Ein Abend in den Ferien" (*LL* 60; *OH* 66) reflects on the forgetfulness

of those who were lucky to survive: "Wer fragt noch danach? / Die
Überlebenden leben" (lines 19–20). It reflects also on their false
claims to innocence which society now accepts and honours: "Die
Schuldigen fordern ihre Unschuld / und erhalten sie –" (lines 21–2).
The poem, "Notiz ohne Bedeutung" (*LL* 66; *OH* 44), presents the por-
trait of a typical survivor: he turns up punctually on the soccer field,
he prays to God for a lottery win and ducks his head at the mention
of the ghetto in Warsaw:

> (Getto von Warschau … ja, richtig, davon hatte er
> flüchtig gehört)
> und er zog den Kopf ein.
> Zur rechten Zeit stand er auf dem Fußballplatz.
> Zur rechten Zeit füllt er seinen Totozettel aus
> und bittet den lieben Gott, den er für so etwas noch braucht,
> er möchte ihn gewinnen lassen. (Lines 13–19)

His occasional insight and the feeling that he had the responsibility to
do something were overlaid by his convenient acceptance of authority:

> Manchmal dachte er,
> es sei nicht alles in Ordnung,
> …
> und er dachte, er müsse –
> aber dann hatte er es vergessen,
> zuviel hatte er schon gemußt, und sein Bedürfnis nach Freiheit
> war gering. (Lines 1–2; 5–8)

Again, Bauer resorts to religious imagery to give voice to his disgust:
"Er wußte nicht, daß Gott / ihn längst ausgespien hatte" (lines 20–1).
  A "Mitläufer"-portrait of a different kind is drawn in the poem "Der
Baum steht noch," (*LL* 63; "Botschaften"). Amid increasingly outspo-
ken criticism, it offers a kinder gesture, an attempt to teach rather than
criticize. The speaker describes, in the third person, his own fate as an
example of what happens to a man who lacks the necessary power of
resistance: unaccustomed or unable to say "no," he went along, not
knowing that he had thereby allowed his back to be broken:

> Weil er niemals ein Nein gesprochen,.
> Haben sie ihm das Rückgrat gebrochen.
> Und er wußte es nicht. (Lines 1–3)

Gradually he began to wonder ("Und er wunderte sich," line 6), and
to gain an idea of what was happening to him ("Und er ahnte es,"

line 9); but before he knew that his life had been shattered, he was hanged (line 11). The speaker finally identifies himself as the "he" of his story (line 13) and bids the "wanderer," to whom he has told his story, not to tarry by the tree that "still stands" there as a monument to past failure: "Verweile nicht, Wanderer. Gott erspare es dir. / Halte dich brav" (lines 14–15.)

The intended message seems to be this: in order for you to be spared my fate, learn from it and act accordingly. God is again invoked, together with the traditional figure of the wanderer. Bauer is here aiming for intensity, but in so doing he avoids the critical issue of his time by incorporating it into the long-established pattern of human thought and sensibility, and by placing God's grace before personal responsibility.

Written in a similar vein of gentle, generalized didacticism is the short poem "Hier zu sein" (LL 64; OH 30). It recalls the time-honoured twin themes of *vanitas mundi* and *carpe diem* and formulates an appeal, "so [zu] leben, / daß wir mit einem Lachen fortgehn," lines 10–11); an appeal to enjoy and appreciate what life offers in full awareness of the transience of all: "und streu die großen Namen mit leichter Hand in die Luft / wie Asche" (lines 16–17).

While these two hortative pieces indicate that Bauer's disenchantment had descended neither into cynicism nor despair, they do not hide a sense of deep resignation encroaching and getting the upper hand – much like the desert in the poem "Aufbau" (LL 67; OH 57), last of the critical European poems included in *Lebenslauf*. As restoration and construction of buildings for residence, entertainment, and all-important bureaucracy are in full swing,

Die Städte werden wieder aufgebaut,
beschädigte Häuser instand gesetzt,
...
Neue Kinos werden gebaut,
mächtige Gebäude für Beamte errichtet, (lines 1–2; 6–7);

as technology progressively facilitates access to the farthest reaches of the globe, eventually to strip the world of all its remaining secrets: "Bald wird jedermann, sein Brot kauend, jede Ferne übersehen. / Bald wird man ohne jedes Geheimnis leben" (lines 10–11); the desert, too, is growing and will soon reach the cities, "singend ihr Triumphlied des Nichts ohne Mitleid" (line 16). The generalization effected by the desert image is exploited to the full by the poem's conclusion: "Denn leicht hat es die Wüste – / sie war schon überall, ehe sie kam" (lines 17–18). The "desert," nothingness without compassion and also nothingness meted out without compassion (line 16), has always bedevilled the social scene and will continue to do so, regardless of any attempt to ward it off. Pointless, therefore, is all criticism and appeal. This poem lays bare one compelling reason for Bauer's break with the "cities" besieged and conquered by the "desert."

The last poem in this group, "Die Wohnung verlassend" (LL 68), documents laconically his final farewell:

> Feste finden in diesen Räumen nicht mehr statt,
> sie sind leer,
> Gespräche haben für immer ihr Ende gefunden. (Lines 1–3)

There will be no more festivities in these rooms, no more conversations. However, significant uncertainties surrounding this fateful step are indicated by the two questions the speaker asks himself. First, "ein Schlußstrich wurde gezogen – / wirklich mit ganz fester Hand?" (lines 11–12). Secondly, "Die Tür ist offen. / Doch was ist hinter der Tür?" (lines 16–17). There is doubt about the completeness of the break with his old "home," and there is caution as to what lies ahead. As I shall show later, Bauer was never to succeed in shaking off this uncertainty.

Looking over the poems that were selected to offer Bauer's post war "report," one may conclude that formal variety continued to be a factor in his choice of texts for his representative *Lebenslauf*. Of the eleven pieces in question, two are openly autobiographical: one expansive and unashamedly emotional ("Ich bin dein Sohn, Europa"), the other concise and factual, controlled even in the expression of disquieting uncertainty ("Die Wohnung verlassend"). One of the critical poems allows an autobiographical reading, too ("Zu meiner Zeit"), but the implied "Personalunion" of poet and speaker is not intended to be vehicle of personal expression so much as to furnish an authentic voice speaking for all those who shared the experience of "my time," be it before or after the war. Explicit criticism points its finger either by means of an emphatic "I"/"they" or "we"/"they" opposition ("Notiz"; "Ein Abend in den Ferien"), or of a negative "he"-portraiture with its implicit claim to typical representation ("Notiz ohne Bedeutung"). Where no such deictic force is mustered, phrase repetition serves to hammer home the point ("Aufbau"). A subtler vehicle of criticism is a dramatic scene, identified as such only by the title, quotation marks enclosing the entire poem, and a concluding turn of phrase giving away the implied dialogue structure ("Einem Fremden etwas zeigend"). Where the speaker's superior knowledge crystallizes in an appeal rather than in criticism, an inclusive "we" is used, acknowledging fellowship in the fragile boat of human life ("Hier zu sein"). Traditional imagery and biblical reference serve as a preamble in this poem to a plea for meaningful appreciative living. However, elaborate rhetoric and emotionalism make its seventeen lines into a construct of limited appeal. Only one poem abandons free verse in favour of a regular metric structure, with verse length and rhyme scheme, repetition and variation working hand in hand to bring out the progression of the speaker's own story, told in order to instruct by negative example ("Der Baum steht noch"). The didacticism of this piece is enhanced by an easily recognizable allusion to Annette von Droste-Hülshoff's *Judenbuche*, woven into the associative texture of the poem to borrow the moral authority of this well known novella. The traditional garb is certainly appealing, but a poem such as "Morgens," time-specific in its frame of reference and less laboured structurally, seems better suited to engage its reader in a thought-provoking imaginative encounter.

⇥ *"Was geschieht, geht mich an."*

Bauer had placed the above motto on his desk for daily contemplation. The poems examined so far confirm the relevance of these words to his writing. As a poet, he set out to "record" his reactions to facts, facets and tendencies of his time, assuming the role of a critical conscience bent upon teaching, helping, healing. For this effect, a variety of approaches, forms, and devices were used, which, on the one hand, testify to the young poet's nascent mastery of his craft, and, on the other, signal the maturing poet's failure to find a distinctive voice that could be recognized and appreciated. The free verse and narrative style he adopted as his principal vehicle of poetic testimony and criticism are extremely difficult to handle effectively, and his tendency to resort to rhetoric for order and intensity could not hope to produce results that consistently appealed to his reader then or now. Some poems offer glimpses of a powerful expressiveness the poet had at his disposal. This, however, was often drowned out by the broader and louder sounds of epic and rhetorical amplification. Bauer must have realized that the impasse in which he eventually found himself could not be blamed solely on the literary scene and its disagreeable ways. It seems fair to assume that when he left Germany "for the sake of his work," he did so not only to free himself from the stifling "Netz papierner Literaturmacherei," but also to create for himself a *tabula rasa* that would allow a poetic renewal.

... And the New

"Besser hier, wo mir niemand auf die Füße tritt.
Besser hier, wo die Chance, die ich noch vor mir sehe,
mir meinen eigenen Atemraum schafft. Besser hier –
auf Gedeih und Verderb."

(Tagebuch 66, 23. November 1976)

CHAPTER FOUR

The Price of Immigration

⊰ *"Doch erst von Euren Enkeln einer wird ...
hier zu Hause sein."*

Bauer's emigration did indeed give fresh nourishment to his disaffected muse, if only by furnishing brand-new subject matter. Poems about the new country, about immigrants from various parts of Europe, about the immigrant Walter Bauer, appropriately begin the Canadian half of his *Lebenslauf.*

It has been suggested that Bauer's image of Canada, before and after immigration, was essentially "a myth of hope and longing, akin to the archetypal search for the promised land" (Riedel, "*Kanadabild*" 197). A similar argument maintains that Bauer's search for a pure, untainted "counter-world" ("Gegenwelt") to the Germany he had left behind ultimately led him to see such an "ideal world" ("Idealwelt") in Canada (Maczewski, *Wanderer* 147; 151). Both positions ascribe to the poet an idealizing perception of the New World. A fresh look at Bauer's Canada poems will yield further insight into his view of the land in which he chose to make a new start. What strikes one on first examination is the small number of poems dealing with his new-found "ideal world." If Canada enabled this disappointed European to satisfy imaginatively his lifelong yearning and vision, why then did he, a writer given to prolixity, devote only five relatively short poems to this pivotal concern of his? The texts themselves, intriguingly reticent in this regard, invite a careful rereading.

Maczewski and Riedel cite three "Canada-poems": "Canada" (*NT* 7), "Kanada" (Maczewski, *Yearbook* 152, by courtesy of Henry Beissel), and "Die Sonne hier muß eine andere sein" (*NT* 26–7). I would add "Ungeheuer von Norden" (*LL* 87; *The Price of Morning* 62) and "Kommt, sagt diese Erde" (*NT* 55). The latter two do not explicitly mention Canada, but as in "Die Sonne ..." the reference is obvious.

Of the Canada poems that have to date received critical attention, only "Canada" has found its way into *Lebenslauf* (70). Maczewski's sensitive interpretation of this piece offers a wealth of insight and explanation. It argues convincingly that the "here-there" contrast presented in the first seven lines of the poem in essence gives voice to Bauer's criticism of Europe ("Europa-Kritik") and related historical and cultural pessimism (*"Geschichts- und Kulturpessimismus,"* 145), and that the subsequent sixteen lines set against this European cultural pessimism a nature optimism (*"Naturoptimismus,"* 146) spawned by the immigrant's hope-filled identification with his host land.

I would suggest that the poem possesses a fine complexity that allows various readings. In its major section, the earth, the wind, the forests, and the rivers deliver their sobering message to the newcomer: your presence here, as was that of those who came before you, is just a fleeting moment in this vast continuum and flux, do not pour too much energy into trying to be part of it:

Diese Erde sagt:
Ich war hier, lange, ehe du kamst und deinesgleichen,
Ungestört sprach ich mit den Winden und Flüssen, vergiß das nicht,
     Freund. –
Der Wind weht kalt von Labrador:
Ich habe eine Botschaft aus der Eiszeit für dich,
Aber ich entziffere sie nicht für dich. –
Die Wälder des Nordens rollen wie Wogen:
Wir werden länger dauern als du. –
Yukon und Mackenzie fließen in ruhiger Geduld:
Sohn, mach es dir nicht zu schwer, andere Zeiten werden nach dir
     kommen, flüchtiger Fremder. – (St. ii, lines 3–12)

While the terms of address used by the earth ("friend," lines 1–5) and the rivers ("son," line 12) imply an inherent benevolence towards the person so addressed, he is, and will remain, a "flüchtiger Fremder" (line 12) – a stranger, in the dual sense of being a fugitive and a transient. Nature thus advising him does not present herself as an entirely gracious hostess opening her arms to receive the culture-weary European immigrant. And as the poem concludes, the sum total of *all* wisdom (my emphasis: wisdom accorded both by culture [first stanza] and nature [second stanza]) is silence: "Aus der Arktis kommt die Endsumme aller Weisheit: / Schweigen. Nichts weiter: Schweigen. Das Ende der Zeit" (st. ii, lines 13–14).

Such "Schweigen," best rendered as "saying nothing" ("Nicht-Sprechen" Maczewski, *Wanderer* 149), will be the "Botschaft aus der Eiszeit") brought to the stranger from Labrador by the icy wind, purposely and appropriately undeciphered (st. II, lines 6–8). "Schweigen" will also be the comprehending recipient's response to the wind's cryptic message.

The reading suggested here, in conjunction with Maczewski's, points up an intriguing ambivalence in Bauer's attitude towards his host land. As Maczewski explains, the wind's explicit refusal may be taken as an offering to the immigrant ("Angebot" 146), an invitation to redefine his position in the overall scheme of life, which in turn will provide him with the cognitive basis for a new beginning (146). I would add that the poem, at once yielding such an opening to a new beginning and declaring "wisdom" to signify the end of speech and history, both opens and closes the door. The possibility of purity ("Reinheit" Maczewski 149) and absolution ("Freispruch" 149) – the object of Bauer's lifelong search and yearning – is here indicated, but located in the realm of Arctic nothingness outside the temporal and spatial bounds of Western culture. A sense of mythical awe, to which Hermann Boeschenstein has drawn our attention (Maczewski 146), informs these lines from first to last, enhancing their thought-provoking ambivalence.

"Kommt, sagt diese Erde" (LL 75) tells us much the same. Again, in Bauer's manner of dramatization, "this earth" is speaking, this time to all those who have come in pursuit of their various desires – "day labourers, gamblers, hoarders, and dreamers" (line 5):

Kommt alle, ich nehme euch willig auf,
Ich gewähre euch alles, was ihr wünscht, viel oder wenig
…
Jeder empfängt hier, was ihm zukommt.
Aber ihr gehört nicht zu mir, ihr seid Fremde,
Ich nehme euch nicht an. (Lines 1–2; 6–8)

They are all welcome, they will all be given what they desire and deserve (line 6) – but they will be treated with indifference (line 9) and denied the gift of closeness and belonging: "But you are not part of me, you are strangers" (line 7). Needless to point out that feeling "alien" ("fremd") in a host country that was not hostile was the essence of Bauer's own experience of Canada. As this poem explains, subtly but unmistakably, the cause of this distressing distance is found in the immigrant's own continued inner connection to his place of origin:

> In euren Kindern wird Europa langsam verhallen,
> Langsam zieh ich sie zu mir, und dann
> Noch einmal, bitterer nun, werdet ihr einsam sein.
> Doch erst von euren Enkeln einer
> Wird das Lied meiner unendlichen Horizonte singen
> Und hier zu Hause sein. (Lines 14–19)

That elusive sense of being at home will take two generations to grow, and will, on a very personal level, only sharpen the edge of the isolation haunting the immigrants of the first generation. The painful experience of increasing rather than diminishing estrangement is, of course, a cultural process. But nature, too, offers little relief. Her sounds instill fear in the newcomers, her silence terrifies them. This is clearly implied by these lines:

> Doch erst von euren Enkeln einer
> ...
> Er wird die Melodie meiner Flüsse verstehen, ohne sich zu
>   fürchten,
> Und die große Sprache meines Schweigens verstehen, die
>   euch erschreckte. (Lines 17; 20–1)

"This earth" will open herself only to the rare individual among their grandchildren's generation who understands and "loves" her: "Ihm erst werde ich seine Liebe belohnen, / Ihm werde ich sagen, wer ich bin" (lines 22–3).

Laying the blame at the immigrant's own door, Bauer's pessimistic assessment of his chances for a successful new beginning does not, of course, rule out a more optimistic view of the New World. However, such optimism, where expressed, is significantly modified by its functional use as a counterpoint to the "Europa-Kritik" which in all of the relevant poems remains Bauer's central concern. The short poem "Ungeheuer von Norden" (LL 87) resumes Bauer's favoured theme of Arctic winds bearing "Botschaften ... von riesiger ... Freiheit" and "unmenschlicher Einsamkeit" (lines 3–4). These being "spring storms" (line 2), they are more than just messengers, they are terrifying agents of nature ("Ungeheuer" von Norden / Kamen die Stürme des Frühjahrs," lines 1–2), setting to work towards a cleansing of the land inhabited by human culture:

Sie rissen alles, alles in Licht,

...

Alles ganz neu und brennend im Licht der Stürme –
O erster vollkommener Tag! – (Lines 10; 14–15)

When the storms subside, everything is as it was before because – the concluding line spells it out – "Wo nichts zu reinigen ist, wehen die Stürme umsonst" (line 17). The unspoken, yet powerfully present final word here is a pointer to the continent "wo alles zu reinigen ist," where everything needs to be cleansed and where such cleansing storms would not do their work in vain.

Clearly, the image of Canada here projected is a distortion of reality (Beissel, DS 6). It has to do with Bauer's continued preoccupation with the there and then of Europe and his consequent disinterest in either a realistic or an idealizing portrayal of Canada. This is borne out by Maczewski's discussion and criticism of the poem "Die Sonne hier" (*Wanderer* 139–43). As to the poem "Kanada," I submit that rather than rendering the exemplary coexistence in Canada of civilization and nature (Maczewski, *Wanderer* 149–50), it points up the contrast between progress-driven urban life and the immutable stillness of nature. This contrast is brought out sharply by the close proximity of these two entirely dissimilar realms (Arend 39). The underlying impetus, it seems to me, is a critical one. Social criticism is indeed the concern of a good number of poems written in Canada; these will be dealt with in a separate chapter.

Bauer's Canada poems give voice to the immigrant poet's rather low-key appraisal of the chances offered to him by his chosen land. To be sure, a measure of optimism and hope must have drawn, impelled, and sustained him. By the evidence of these poems, however, optimism and hope were heavily overlaid with a sobering awareness of his own continued intellectual and emotional bondage to the Old World which rendered him incapable of merging with the New.

> *"Der Jemand war, wird Niemand,*
> *und er hält es nicht für wahr."*

The two poems to be considered next present straight autobiography, giving a plain-spoken, first-person account of the immigrant Bauer's motivations and hopes, of his views and insights a few years after his arrival. These pieces clarify and expand, with the authority of the personal voice and the immediacy of actual experience, what the dramatically structured Canada poems could only intimate about the tensions at work in this immigrant's mind.

"Fortgegangen von meinem Vaterland" (LL 71–2; NT 13–14) may be described as an intellectual stock-taking five years after emigration. The keynote of this agonized but sober self-examination is tension: tension between hope, signalled by his departure from home, and misgivings about the existence anywhere of what he had set out to find:

Fortgegangen von meinem Vaterland,
Um etwas zu finden, was es vielleicht nicht gab,
Nie geben würde, nirgendwo, für keinen, der fortging. (Lines 1–3)

Tension informs his despairing search for a healthy and confident mind:

Krank von meinem Versagen von zuviel Ausflucht, Beschönigung,
    Selbstbeschwichtigung, von zuviel von allem,
Verzweifelnd suchend nach Gesundheit, Hoffnung in mir wie
    einen blassen Keim. (Lines 10–11)

There is tension between his idealistic perseverance and his knowledge of its doubtful success: "Suchend noch immer mit der Narrheit eines Sohnes von Don Quixote" (line 20); and the tension of perceiving himself as a stranger among people whom he considers as his brothers: "Ein Fremder unter ihnen, mit denen ich nichts als die Zeit teilte, / Und jeder von ihnen mein Bruder" (lines 21–2).

The poem ends with an affirmation, derived from experience and reflection, of such inner conflict as the necessary incentive for the new start the immigrant has set out to make: "Denn ich weiß es nun, am Grunde muß man anfangen, / für sich selbst, ein verzweifelt hoffender Einzelner" (lines 24–5). And for the "record" as much as for personal reassurance, this is where I, the immigrant Walter Bauer, began: "Und dort fing ich an" (line 26).

"Von abends sieben bis morgens vier" (LL 73; NT 11) describes in terse but powerful language and imagery the physically and mentally taxing nightshift which was Bauer's own beginning "at the bottom," with its share of loneliness, desperation, and hope never quite extinguished. The poem's subtext clearly goes beyond autobiography and offers insight into the process by which the hard facts of the immigrant's experience drain him of his initial enthusiasm and drive.

In the beginning his dreams are fresh, his visions of himself as a master of the world intact: "Um neun sind die Träume noch frisch und leuchten, / Und ich könnte die ganze Welt besser einrichten, als sie ist" (lines 5–6). As time goes by, as it deals up the constraints of reality rather than a fulfilment of the promises it seemed to hold, disenchantment sets in and gives rise to a growing sense of paralysing futility and failure, of life gone to waste:

Um Mitternacht schleppt sich die Zeit durch den dampfigen Raum
Und legt sich verendend zu meinen Füßen.
Um zwei erinnere ich mich kaum noch an etwas
Und wische die Reste meines Lebens
In die Abfalltonne. (Lines 7–11)

Again, Bauer's depressing reflections culminate in a positive turn provided by the concluding image of the milky way allowing him, moments before its own extinction, a drink of "liberation":

"Um vier trete ich in den scharfen einsamen Wind
Und trinke, eh sie erlöscht,
Aus der Milchstraße Befreiung" (lines 14–16).

Yet the affirmative touch at the end of this poem, as that at the end of "Fortgegangen von meinem Vaterland," does nothing to alleviate the overall pained tenor of these reflections on the poet's own immigrant experience. While such a concluding gesture indicates a mind willing to face up to the challenge, the mood of this mind remains somber and far removed from any unmitigated optimism.

Prime witness in this regard is the poem "Politischer Emigrant" (LL 110). Strictly speaking, it is not a personal account. The label "political," however, and the third person of the persona, provide only a thin veneer to protect Bauer's own self from direct exposure. He clearly considered his role as a writer and poet to be of social significance and in that sense "political." The poet, no less than the politician, is a representative (st. I, line 2) and a leader (st. II, line 1) of many. His reason for emigrating, as that of the politician, is a matter of the mind ("Hoffnungen," st. I line 2) rather than the material need driving away other "Auswanderer" from home (LL 69; for a discussion of this poem see p. 67). It seems safe to assume that the observation, the unmasking, and the criticism voiced in the five stanzas of "Politischer Emigrant" have as their object the "political emigrant" Walter Bauer and formulate an honest, distressing appraisal of his own situation.

The major charge levelled here against himself is that of self-delusion. Delusion is the true face of his energizing assumption that his emigration will serve a need larger than his own, while in reality it removes him from the sole arena where he could be of use to those whom he wishes to serve: "Wer flieht, der nimmt sich selbst aus der Geschichte aus, / Indes er glaubt, er nähm' die Hoffnungen von vielen mit" (st. I, lines 1–2). This is to say, the poet's voice, Bauer's voice, calling from abroad will not be heard, let alone be heeded, by those who have stayed at home, shrugging their shoulders and accommodating themselves as best as they can (st. II, lines 1–2). Delusion, again, is the true face of his reassuring rationalization "Sein kommt vor Bewußtsein" (st. II, line 3) – a commonplace, neat and trivial, cited to sharpen the double-edged self-criticism: "O Täuschung, die er jeden Tag erfrischt, um noch zu leben!" (st. II, line 4). "Fortgegangen von meinem Vaterland" has already given an idea of Bauer's "Bewußtsein," his subjection to memory, guilt, and shame which haunted him like a ghost. The present poem states with greater detachment, yet by no means lesser force of conviction and persuasion, the futility of such carefully nurtured "Täuschung":

Erwartungen, sorgsam gepflegt, um sich des Grunds nicht zu berauben,
O Hoffnung auf – doch zahlt sie sich nicht aus,
Denn Hoffnung dieser Art schmeckt ihm zuletzt wie altes Brot in
    fremdem Licht,
Und was er sagt, beklagt, beschwört, verstehn die andern nicht. (St. III)

To rub even more salt into the wound, the following stanza goes into expressive detail. The disappointed immigrant indulges in imaginative scenes of liberation from grief, but nobody hears or cares, and soon he, too, will be a nobody, but one who clings to the shadow of his greatness:

Er spielt sich auf der leeren Szene selbst Befreiung vor,
Bald wird kein Hund ihm noch ein "Ich hör zu" für seine Trauer geben.
Der Jemand war, wird Niemand, und er hält es nicht für wahr.

(St. IV, lines 2–4)

No alleviating turn or suggestion is found at the end of this poem. Instead, a factual and depressing summation: perpetually branded as an "emigrant" (st. V, line 3; see below), he remains firmly attached to his origins; neither the next generation (line 2) nor history at large (line 4) will recognize him: all identifying traces – who he was, when and where he lived (lines 2; 5) – will have been "blown away" (line 5):

> Und so im Warten auf was niemals kommt, ergraut sein Haar.
> Auch kommen Jüngere: "Wer? Wann?" und: "Hierorts unbekannt."
> In seinem Paß wird nie gelöscht, woher er kam und: Emigrant.
> Geschichte lacht nicht und bedauert nicht: sie geht.
> Mit dürr gewordener Saat der alte Sämann: wo? Verweht. (St. v)

The sower who leaves his land will commit his seeds to the wind and himself to oblivion.

"Politischer Emigrant," placed in *Lebenslauf* in the chronological context of the early sixties, tells us in no uncertain terms that Bauer's assessment of his emigration, which he undertook in the hope of finding the opportunity to recharge his creative batteries and pave the way to social/historical significance, was a clear admission of failure.

⊰ *"Canada ist ein gutes Wort."*

Having sampled the frankness and rigour of Bauer's self-criticism, one is struck not only by the calm and detached tone of his reflections on other immigrants' lives, but also by a significant shift of viewpoint. The poems "Lebenslauf I" (*LL* 76) and "Lebenslauf II" (*LL* 77) feature two immigrants, hailing from Greece and the Ukraine respectively, whose names change from Odysseus to Bill and from Gregory to Georgie and signal these men's pragmatic attempts to pull up their foreign roots and adapt to the soil of the host culture. What factors of foreignness or estrangement are found to exist in their new lives have to do with other people's perception, not their own. In Bill's case, it is his Canadian-born children who have no connection to the life and culture of their father's native land, largely because of the comforts they enjoy in their own:

> Seine Kinder, auf kanadischer Erde geboren,
> wußten nichts mehr von Telemach
> oder Penelope, die den Schleier der Erwartung spann,
> und das Wehen der Ahornbäume im Indian Summer
> war ihnen lieber
> als das scharfe Licht über dem attischen Marmor,
> der nicht satt macht. ("Lebenslauf I," lines 15–21)

As for Georgie, a political emigrant, Canada has offered him rest ("Ruhe") which he could find neither at home nor elsewhere in Europe:

> Revolutionen
> hatten ihn von einem Land zum andern getrieben.
> Zu oft hatte er Wurzeln in fremde Erde gesenkt
> und geglaubt, nun könnte er bleiben.
> Stürme dann, an denen er schuldlos war,
> wehten ihn weiter
> und schließlich über das Meer.
> Seine Heimat war Saporoshje,
> aber hier hatte er Ruhe. ("Lebenslauf ii," lines 1–9)

Only his face and his general bearing suggest, to an outside observer, the "Russian" that he was:

> Nur das Gesicht noch
> war Erde von russischer Erde,
> und wenn er ging, langsam, bedächtig
> (auch wenn die Arbeit eilig war),
> sah er aus, als ginge er
> über ein Sommerfeld der Ukraine. (Lines 10–15)

The third "Lebenslauf" (LL 78), too, reflects on an immigrant's apparently successful transformation. It tells of a Jewish death-camp survivor from Hungary whose face dropped suddenly when she learned of her streetcar companion's German identity and who, sometime later, was able to greet him with a smile:

> Vielleicht war dies die Frucht
> friedlicher kanadischer Sommer
> und eines Zimmers, in dem sie endlich
> für sich war. (Lines 27–30)

Her change of heart may have been the "fruit" of peaceful Canadian summers, the speaker speculates, or of the privacy she at long last enjoyed in a room of her own. Again, Canada with its congenial conditions is given the credit.

These three "Lebensläufe" attest to Bauer's keen awareness and appreciation of what this hospitable country had to offer and could do for its immigrants. They attest also to his profound humaneness which prompted him to view the other people in the immigrant boat with sympathetic friendliness, while his equally profound honesty inclined him towards uncompromising self-analysis and criticism. As Henry Beissel confirmed recently, Bauer "vermied [es], andere zu verurteilen. Aber mit sich selbst ging er erbarmungslos ins Zeug" (*Sonnentanz* 223). Where he was moved to criticize his fellow immigrants, he took care to soften his charge with a large infusion of compassion. The poem "Auswanderer" (*LL* 69; *OH* 75) serves to illustrate this point. It is a fine blend of cold criticism and warm understanding of the emigrants on board the "Argentina" *en route* to the New World. By emigrating they managed to escape the relentless sun and the boundless poverty of Sicily: "der afrikanischen Sonne Siziliens waren sie entflohen / und grenzenloser Armut" (lines 3–4). They have freed themselves from natural and social conditions to which no one can wish to be subjected. However, their eyes betray "hopes" that horrify the knowing observer:

> Hoffnungen ... ungeheurer Art:
> Studebaker oder Buick,
> Eisschrank, Radio, ein Haus
> und immer zu essen. (Lines 15–18)

One will naturally sympathize with these poor creatures who can only dream of the material comfort afforded by a Studebaker or a Buick, by a refrigerator, a radio, a house, by food whenever it is wanted. But their hopes are "ungeheuer" to the onlooker, disquieting, because – here the reader is invited to speculate – his vision, unobstructed by the circumstances blocking theirs, allows him to look further afield and anticipate their disenchantment and/or their enslavement to the God called "money." This is what in Bauer's style the poem's conclusion brings into sharp focus: "Und wie eine messianische Botschaft / hörte man immer wieder ein Wort: / money" (lines 23–5). "Like a messianic call," the word "money" was heard without end. Money, the prime mover, lures these unfortunate souls from the material poverty of their native country to the spiritual poverty of North American materialism. It seems impossible to separate the criticism from the compassion, and therein lies the particular appeal of this poem.

> *"Mit Leidenschaft und mit Vernunft,*
> *mit [dem] Herzen und mit genauer Hand."*

One need not enter into a detailed analysis of the ten Canadian poems considered in this chapter to realize that Bauer, when he emigrated, took with him almost all of the formal devices he had gathered and experimented with during the years of his poetic apprenticeship and mature practice in Europe. What he appears to have left behind are the all too obvious metric forms of regular stanza, rhythm, and rhyme. Only remnants are found, albeit concentrated, in the emotionally laden piece "Politischer Emigrant" where stanzaic organization (four 4-line units and a 5-line conclusion) and regular rhythmic alternation seem to have been called upon to aid in the distancing of insights hurtful to the poet's own mind and heart. Rhymes, too, have been mustered to link two lines in each stanza (st. I, II, lines 2–3; st. III: lines 3–4; st. IV: lines 1–2), and to provide two concluding couplets in stanza v (see p. 65).

The other poems are free of such traditional formalism. They do, however, reflect Bauer's continuing partiality for rhetorical devices. We find contrast in "Canada"; not "Plato's wisdom" will be received on this continent, but "other wisdom" – "icy and not digestible to everyone":

Diese Erde beschenkt dich nicht
Mit der Weisheit Platons,
Aristoteles lebte hier nicht. (St. I, lines 1–3)

Andere Weisheit empfängst du hier,
Herb und eisig und nicht bekömmlich für jeden. (St. II, lines 1–2)

There is parallelism in "Von abends sieben bis morgens vier," signalled by the hours cited to mark the speaker's mental journey through the night (emphasis added):

Um neun sind die Träume noch frisch und leuchten,
Und ich könnte die ganze Welt besser einrichten, als sie ist. (Lines 5–6)

Um Mitternacht schleppt sich die Zeit durch den dampfigen Raum
Und legt sich verendend zu meinen Füßen. (Lines 7–8)

Um zwei erinnere ich mich kaum noch an etwas
Und wische die Reste meines Lebens
In die Abfalltonne. (Lines 9–11)

Um vier trete ich in den scharfen einsamen Wind
Und trinke, eh sie erlöscht,
Aus der Milchstraße Befreiung. (Lines 14–16)

Repetition and amplification are employed to bring out the confessional intensity of "Fortgegangen von meinem Vaterland":

Fortgegangen von meinem Vaterland,
Um etwas zu finden, was es vielleicht nicht gab,
Nie geben würde, nirgendwo, für keinen, der fortging ... (Lines 1–3)

Fortgegangen von meinem Vaterland,
Beladen mit zuviel Erinnerung an zuviel Tod, vergiftet von Schuld,
Für die ich noch immer, zögernder immer, den Richter suchte ...

(Lines 6–8)

Personification is used in the poem "Kommt, sagt diese Erde," which in its entirety – except for the speaker's minimal interjection "says this earth" in line 1 – is spoken by the earth of the host country, welcoming all her immigrants and telling them what and what not to expect:

Kommt alle, ich nehme euch willig auf,
Ich gewähre euch alles, was ihr wünscht, viel oder wenig ... (Lines 2–3)

Aber ihr gehört nicht zu mir, ihr seid Fremde,
Ich nehme euch nicht an. (Lines 7–8)

Climactic conclusion is found in "Auswanderer": "Und wie eine messianische Botschaft / hörte man immer wieder ein Wort: / money" (lines 23–5).

These poems likewise reflect Bauer's unbroken dramatic bent ("Kommt, sagt diese Erde") and his penchant for variation of perspective (first person: "Fortgegangen von meinem Vaterland"; third person specific: "Lebenslauf I–III"; third person general: "Politischer Emigrant"; direct address: "Canada"; retrospect: "Lebenslauf I–III"; reflection on present: "Von abends sieben bis morgens vier"). But all of this now translates into a more guarded manner of presentation, making the formative effort less obvious and therefore potentially more effective. A carefully crafted, yet apparently unpretentious natural diction, cast in a variety of long and short lines, adds to the readability of these poems. What they do not possess in any significant measure is metaphor (exception: "Von abends sieben ...") and the finesse of indirection and suggestiveness. Bauer, in accordance with the principal article of his poetological faith, spells things out directly, clearly, emphatically, complete down to the last detail or nuance. Some of his readers will feel deprived of the pleasure and challenge of using their own imagination and judgment; others will appreciate the straightforwardness and intelligibility of his poetic "record."

Holding Up the Mirror

🎵 *"Dieser schauerliche Materialismus,*
   hier wie dort."

What has been said about the discriminative targeting of criticism and compassion applies only to the emigrant Bauer commenting on himself and on his fellow emigrants. When it comes to Bauer vis-à-vis his host society at large, the perspective is curiously reversed. While presenting himself, modestly but firmly, as the caring fellow man he no doubt strove to be and was, he found strong words of disapproval and censure for the shallow-minded, money-driven mass around him. The group of poems considered here includes some of his less successful works.

"Zuerst werden wir einen Wagen haben" (*LL* 91; *NT* 49), for example, is a model of heavy-handed moralizing. Its first part (lines 1–8) is structured as a dialogue between one such New-World hedonist and a "Socratic" questioner who, in the second part (lines 9–21), spills out his vexation at how these people fracture and waste their lives. The introductory exchange is one of euphoric anticipation and censorious prompting: "We are going to have a car." – "To be faster than time? Good. And then?" – "An apartment or house." – "To fill with emptiness? Good. And then?" – "Television." – "To lose language? Good. And then?" (lines 1–6). At the point where the born-to-shop enthusiast runs out of specific items to add to the list of things to be acquired, his critical mentor showers him, and the reader, with a litany of facts about souls and hopes and life and wholeness being lost to the God of acquisition on credit. Here is an excerpt:

Gut, was dann? … Wurde nicht etwas vergessen? –
Verlorene Seelen, tot schon lange Zeit,
Tot, ehe sie starben.
Jahr um Jahr zahlten sie ab,

Mit Geld, mit Hoffnungen, mit Jahren,
Das ganze Leben zahlten sie ab, Stück um Stück,
Da war nie etwas Ganzes. (Lines 8–14)

In "Die großen Stürme, so lesen wir" (LL 74; NT 62), the "Tellerwä-scher" Bauer reflects on people's general indifference to upheavals and catastrophes as long as they happen at a safe distance. The conciliatory mask held up at the beginning in the form of an inclusive "we" (lines 1 and 3) is soon dropped in order to distance the speaker critically from "you" (line 7) who think that comfort and security can be bought:

Wie wir lesen, um es wieder zu vergessen,
Richten sie beträchtlichen Schaden an.
…
Doch, was, wenn sie näher kommen,
Was, wenn sie sich zu euch bewegen,
die sich so sicher glaubten
Und alle möglichen Versicherungen abgeschlossen haben,
Einschließlich der mit dem Lenker der Stürme? (Lines 3–4; 6–10)

What, he asks them, will you do if "the big storms" come your way, if they move closer to you who consider yourselves protected by your various insurance policies? The scenario he pictures to himself in answer to his question is one of pitiful whining: you will duck like frightened fowl and be utterly confused (lines 11–12); you will look for a guilty party who failed to guard your "sleep" (lines 13–14); you will lament the unwonted deprivation and the loss of insurances and payments that were to secure your future (lines 16–18). In a surprise turn, the speaker, employed to wash dishes for these people, reminds himself of his own dependence on them, and thus also on the safe distance of those "storms." The terror the storms unleash will blunt people's appetites, and dishwashers will not be needed:

Wenn die großen Stürme kommen,
Werden viele Leute die Lust am Essen verlieren,
Dann wird man kaum jemanden noch brauchen,
Der Teller wäscht.
So sind auch wir im Grunde
Von der Ferne oder Nähe der Stürme abhängig.
Möchten die Stürme nicht zu früh kommen.
Aber warum sollten sie nicht kommen? (Lines 21–8)

The accuser, struck by the precariousness of his own situation, finds himself reduced to hoping – not unlike those he has just accused – that the storms may not come too soon (line 27). His response to the apparent dilemma is a rhetorical question: "But why should they not come?" (line 28). It serves to express his own sense of helplessness and also to invite the reader to draw his or her own conclusions. Bauer's message here is a word of caution concerning the reliability of any superior insights one may have, and the self-righteous attitude that might come with such insights.

Quite different in kind and effect is the short piece "Siehst du das Herz der Stadt?" (LL 94; KN 19). Rather than spelling out the raw material of thought and accusation, it offers the reader a picture to visualize and interpret. The image is of a construction worker walking home after the day's work, with his young wife at his side and their small son on his shoulders, the latter singing a song that no one understands or even hears:

> Da war ein Mann – wie immer der hieß, den ich traf –
> Ein Bauarbeiter, man konnte es sehen –
> Ein Mann, der abends nach Hause ging;
> Er trug seinen kleinen Sohn auf den Schultern,
> Seine junge Frau ging neben ihnen.
> Der Kleine, erhoben über alle,
> Sang ein Lied, das keiner verstand und niemand hörte.
> Das Herz der Stadt. (Lines 9–16)

This is the counter-image that has returned to the speaker's memory as he ponders the view and the supposed greatness of the gigantic buildings of banks, insurance corporations, and department stores, located in, or constituting what is said to be, "the heart of the city":

> "Siehst du das Herz der Stadt?" sagte jemand zu mir,
> Und er zeigte auf die Banken, wies auf die
> Mächtigen Gebäude der Versicherungskompanien,
> Die Kaufhäuser wie Aladins Wunderhöhlen –
> "Groß, nicht wahr?" – Vielleicht.
> Vielleicht etwas kleiner, vielleicht
> Nicht ganz so groß.
> Das Herz der Stadt ...? (Lines 1–8)

These two contrasting images are juxtaposed in a familiar setting that involves gesture and direct speech. What adds to the fascination of this poetic structure is the fact that the reader cannot determine whether or not the speaker communicates his response – both his thoughts (lines 5–8) and his recollection (lines 9–15) – to the person whose idea of "the heart of the city" he thereby corrects. His own idea, however, is made perfectly clear, as is his criticism that the real heart of the joint human endeavour will neither be recognized nor be understood by those who allow themselves to be dazzled by the edifices of the financial world.

And those whose comprehension is circumscribed by the limited capacity of their utilitarian mind will be incapable of understanding and appreciating things that are valuable for something other than their material usefulness. This sets the odd individual against the mass of people, as the vignette "Guter Fischfang" (LL 98) clearly suggests. It features a fisherman returning after six hours of fishing with a paltry catch of only small fish, but perfectly happy and at one with himself:

Was macht es mir aus. Ich hatte
Sechs Stunden völliger Stille, kann man mir
Nicht ansehen, daß ich
Etwas Unbeschreibliches fing?
Aber ihr wart nicht dabei …
Ihr fragt nach Fischen fürs Abendbrot.
Ich genoß etwas ganz anderes als Mahl und Trunk. (Lines 8–14)

Again Bauer refrains from spelling things out from stating clearly the exact nature of the "indescribable" thing (line 11) the fisherman caught during the six hours of "complete stillness" (line 9) on the lake. While lending his reader a helpful hand, he still leaves it up to him or her to fill this "Leerstelle" according to his or her own light. Furthermore, as in "Siehst du das Herz der Stadt," a positive perspective has been substituted for the negativity of fault finding, resulting in a mode of criticism well suited to the humanist's pen. The biblical and literary associations evoked by the "Fischfang"-image only enhance the charm of this little poem.

Clearly, the criticism voiced by the last two poems is not directed specifically at Canadian or North American society. It is social comment relevant to any prosperous Western society, particularly the "Wohlstandsgesellschaft" in whose language it is written. This is true also of the longer piece "Die Drosseln sterben nicht aus" (LL 95–7), even though the critical focus here has shifted and widened from contemporary money-mindedness and materialism to age-old philistinism still very much alive. The "message" of this poem has already been discussed (see p. 15). At this point, a few words of comment on its peculiar form will be added. Direct and relentless critical statement is laced with imaginatively distancing metaphor, probably in an attempt to combine the expressive power of both types of poetic utterance for optimum effectiveness.

Referring to "the poet," the first line immediately identifies the "thrushes" mentioned in the title as the poem's central metaphor: the bird of song representing the songster among the "nine-to-five-men" and "good housewives" (st. I, lines 6–7). He is hated for being different, for indulging happily in useless song: "Einer sang, während sie sich abschunden, / Um Haus, Wagen, Lebensversicherung zu bezahlen" (st. I, lines 17–18). The first stanza is a lengthy account of the fact that "they" have at last managed to get rid of "him." The thrush image is introduced in the form of a simile which likens the murder they have committed to a boy's cold-blooded killing of a thrush and careless disposal of its body in the bushes:

> Wie der Junge mit seiner Schleuder
> den Flug der Drossel zerbrach, und dann,
> Mit flüchtigem Bedauern,
> Stieß er mit dem Fuß
> Die gestorbenen Lieder ins Gebüsch. (St. I, lines 10–14)

The second stanza picks up the metaphoric thread, but adds immediate explication: sometime later, a scholar was to find, "In the bushes, that is: / In a shabby room / A bundle of papers":

> Später fand ein Gelehrter
> Im Gebüsch, *das heißt*:
> *In einem armseligen Zimmer*
> Ein Bündel Papiere. (St. II, lines 1–4; emphasis added)

We are back to four lines of third-person account informing us what the scholar did with his find. He published these papers, complete with his own annotations to indicate that he had discovered a "dead" poet who had been unfairly ignored in his own time:

> Und ließ sie drucken
> Und versah sie fleißig mit Anmerkungen:
> Er hatte einen toten Poeten entdeckt,
> Mißachtet von seiner Zeit, (St. II, lines 5–8)

This is followed by six lines of reported speech rendering those good people's predictably confused response. We knew it, they said, there had been something special in his [the dead poet's] voice. But why couldn't he be like us? He could have made a decent living:

> Da haben wir es, sagten sie,
> Wir wußten, da war etwas,
> Etwas ganz Besonderes in seiner Stimme.
> Nur: warum war er nicht wie wir,
> Brav von neun bis fünf?
> Er hätte sein gutes Auskommen gehabt. – (St. ii, lines 9–14)

The concluding three lines return to the level of metaphor to throw into relief the speaker's comment:

> Die Haustiere sagten zur Drossel:
> Leb ohne Flügel,
> Ersticke deine Stimme. (St. ii, lines 15–17)

Stanza iii resumes the line of narrative account devoid of figurative indirection, describing how these philistines erected a monument in honour of the dead poet. In stanza iv a "real" thrush enters the picture: it is reported to have settled occasionally on the poet's statue, singing into the "dead" ear of the "dead" figure:

> Manchmal dann,
> …
> Setzte sich eine Drossel
> Auf seine Schulter
> und sang dem Toten
> Ins tote Ohr. (St. iv, lines 1; 4–7)

Stanza v continues the direct account structure: a young person finds the long forgotten poems and hails their author as his model and friend. Stanza vi, like stanza ii, ends in the newly resumed metaphoric strain, putting – much to the puzzlement of this reader – the metaphor into the mouths of those accused of philistine intolerance and distaste for artful expression: "Hier ist, sagen sie, / Kein Platz für Drosseln" (st. vi, lines 5–6). Stanza vii is an epigrammatic summation by the speaker: "But the thrushes / do not die out." It repeats the wording of the title and thus closes the poem's metaphoric frame. Beside such shifting and mixing of account and figuration, the poem relies heavily on reported speech and repetition, giving rise also to some doubt as to the wisdom of making the "nine-to-five-men" and "good housewives" formulate, in thought or word, the question "why was he not like us, / well behaved from nine to five?" (st. II, lines 12–13).

Bauer's desire to communicate his ideas clearly also undermines, here and there, the considerable expressive power of a well crafted poem, "Guernica: Undeutliche Erinnerung" (LL 126–7). Its critical targets are political gullibility and complacency, both thriving on insensitivity and indifference to the concerns and even the lives of others. The word "Guernica" with all its associations allows an effective montage of the history of war (the role of German legionaries in the Spanish Civil War) and the history of art and music (Picasso's painting "Guernica" which depicts the destruction of this city; Casals, the great Bach-mediator and politically responsible cellist who emigrated and thereafter refused to perform in Franco's Spain) to expose the convenient forgetfulness of the older generation and the uncaring ignorance of the young. Structurally, the poem is an ironic blend of factual narration, direct quotation, literary reference, cryptic aside and rhetorical questioning. The potency of this rich mixture, however, is diluted by occasionally redundant explication.

To illustrate the point: the roughly three decades that have passed since the bombing of Guernica (1937) are "centuries" to those who prefer to forget. This plain, if unsettling psychological fact is thrown into sharp critical relief by the pithy *non sequitur*: "1936, vor Jahrhunderten also" (st. I, line 6). A parenthetical explanation is added to clarify that this was centuries ago "as far as memory is concerned" (st. II, line 1). The simple, if slightly varied reiteration of that curious and therefore memorable piece of logic at the conclusion of stanza III, "Vor Jahrhunderten, wie gesagt" (st. III, line 9), seems a much more powerful way of reinforcing a point so easily understood.

Here is another example. The end of the poem explains that young people admire Picasso's "Guernica" strictly from an artistic point of view, because otherwise they have nothing to do with Guernica:

Die jungen Leute bewundern Picassos "Guernica", natürlich nur
Vom rein künstlerischen Standpunkt her, "denn was haben wir",
Sagen sie, "mit Guernica zu tun?" (St. IV, lines 5–7)

This point was made, with graphic poignancy, in the preceding stanza: "Ihre Kinder bewundern Picassos 'Guernica' – / ('Großartig' – 'Erschütternd' – 'Der ganze Schrecken der Zeit') –" (st. III, lines 5–6). Its discursive elaboration, while forming part of the concluding rhetorical summation, gives rise to a sense of unease and overload. As in the poem "Die Drosseln sterben nicht aus," a largely unreflected attitude is formulated to provoke reflection. The provocation seems to misfire, however, due to the heavy-handed way in which the incriminating words are put into the collective mouth of the collectively accused. The cloak of objectivity borrowed from the detached third-person account does nothing to cover the naked self-righteousness of such finger pointing; nor does the speaker's concluding rhetorical question – "Und was eigentlich war Guernica?" (st. IV, line 8) serve to weaken this impression.

⅔ "Hütet euch."

A poetic structure Bauer came to use more and more, with skill and success, is that of a cycle or sequence of short poems of varying content and form strung together as one thought or observation gives rise to another. While the individual pieces may stand and be considered on their own, they are bound by an inner connecting thread that enhances their profile and sharpens their bite. "Nichts ist schlimmer als Frieden" (LL 105–8) will serve as an example. It is a critical reaction to various facets and ramifications of the United States' involvement in Vietnam.

In the first poem, the communicative format of a letter is indicated. The writer's introductory remark about his reluctance to make mention, again, of the New York Stock Exchange (st. I, lines 1–3) suggests prior communication. He does mention it because news of impending peace has caused, again, a sudden decline in prices (lines 4–7). In a second stanzaic unit, he quotes questions apparently raised by concerned customers at that volatile financial institution. In the third unit he offers his conclusion, using the words that also serve as the title. Clearly marked "PS.," a postscript is added to report that there is no longer need to worry, the news about peace turned out to be a false rumour, the stock exchange is well again:

> P.S.
> Kein Grund zur Beunruhigung:
> Die Nachrichten vom kommenden Frieden
> Haben sich als Enten herausgestellt.
> Der Krieg geht weiter,
> Der Pulsschlag der Börse ist
> Erfreulicherweise
> Wieder normal. (I: st. IV)

The remarkable thing about the entire poem is its sustained ironic stance – a critical weapon rarely used by Walter Bauer.

Poems II and III continue the implied report structure, although one cannot determine clearly whether the underlying format is that of a letter, of an account without a specific addressee, or of the writer communicating with himself. Such formal ambiguity serves effectively to draw the reader in, to sharpen his or her sensors, to heighten curiosity and desire to properly decode the message.

While poem I takes aim at various financial interest groups reaping profit from the war, poem II calls attention to the inhumanity of the head count conducted along with the killing: "Es heißt, daß nun auf jeden / Getöteten Vietkong sechs Zivilisten kommen" (II: st. I, lines 4–5). Poem III directs its critical gaze at the newspapers and their dubious claim to report nothing but the whole truth: "die reine Wahrheit und nichts als / die Wahrheit" (lines 2–3). Ironic quotation is again employed to point up sharply the intended message. Another stratagem of reader involvement is the unanswered question at the end of the first stanza"Was meine ich, wenn ich / Diesen unscheinbaren Vogel erwähne?" (lines 11–12). The "insignificant bird" here referred to is the sparrow who, unlike "hawks, doves [and] ducks" (line 6), is never mentioned in newspaper reports. Thus the reader is invited to recall the fuss about the proponents ("hawks"), the opponents ("doves"), and the evaders ("ducks") of the Vietnam war, while lives lived quietly away from the war effort were "insignificant" and not considered newsworthy. We hear the voice of the humanist whose sympathy has always gone out, first and foremost, to the little people.

The mention of these various animal symbols sparks off in the writer's mind memories of World War I and of children being taught to ridicule the Russian bear, the French cock, the British lion (III: st. II, lines 3–6) – and to be proud of the German eagle (lines 7–8). "Wo ist der Adler nun?" he asks in conclusion (line 9), again inviting his readers to answer and interpret for themselves.

In the next two poems the critical focus narrows to bring into view the killer (IV) and the killed (V). As idealizing clichés would have it, the bomber pilot is doing his duty for the sake of his country and his loved ones, for the protection of democracy and freedom:

Für das Vaterland,
Für die Demokratie,
Für die Verteidigung der Freiheit,
Für [s]eine Lieben daheim. (IV: st. I, lines 2–5)

The speaker, however, corrects the suggestion that these are indeed the pilot's motives. What makes this man do what he does is love of flying, his pride in precision work, his insensitivity to the actual results of his "job well done":

Er liebte das Fliegen,
Er liebte seinen Beruf,
Genugtuung empfand er, wenn
Die Bomben sich lösten, und
Befriedigung über die Präzision des Abwurfs;
Und wie von gut getaner Arbeit
Kehrte er heim ... (IV: st. II, lines 2–8)

But rather than pointing a moral finger at this individual's particular depravity, the speaker, in conclusion, recognizes a universally human force at work: "Aus solchen Höhen allerdings / Sieht man Gesichter nicht mehr" (IV: st. III). Which is to say: if we don't see it, it doesn't affect us – why should we worry? Sobering realism about human nature from the pen of a man who so dearly wanted to love his fellow human beings.

The fifth poem brings the camera down, as it were, to focus on the faces the death-bearing precision worker cannot make out from the heights at which he is operating. Four couplets of parallel structure depict, one by one, ordinary people – a peasant, a mother, a grandfather, a child – all engaged in hope-filled, future-oriented activities just before the bomb came down to say "No." A few lines will serve as illustration:

Kurz ehe der Bauer starb,
Hatte er Furchen gezogen.
Kurz ehe die junge Mutter starb,
Hatte sie ihr Kind gesäugt.
...
Die Bombe sagte:
Nein. (V: st. I, lines 1–4; 9–10)

The absence of any further comment serves as an effective agent of emphasis.

Poem VI returns from the scene of blind precision-killing to the home of its perpetrators. The speaker is explicitly present again, telling us, in a vivid and memorable image, that the New World's ambassadors of freedom are getting a little tired of the ideals held up to inspire their mission elsewhere in the world. The speaker has heard it said that the Statue of Liberty finds it hard to keep holding up the torch:

Ich habe gehört,
Daß der Freiheitsstatue
...

Der Arm vom Heben des Lichtes
Zu schwer wird. (VI: lines 1–5)

"At night," when no one can see it, the lady will lower her arm,
allowing it to rest (lines 7–8). The speaker's concluding gesture of
brushing this aside as a rumour (lines 9–10) serves to underscore
what has been said and implied.

The two short pieces that round off the entire sequence are framed
and thus held together by the warning "Hütet euch" – "Beware"
(VII: line 1; VIII: line 5). The warning voice is that of the concerned
observer who knows from experience what happens on the return of
the "praetorians," the armed guards who will obey orders to kill. He
has seen it all before in Germany, under the reign of the eagle's right
wing. And soon, he warns, the American eagle will lose one wing
and be left with only the right one:

Bald
Wird der amerikanische Adler
Nur noch einen Flügel besitzen:
Den rechten.
Hütet euch. (VIII)

It appears that in the form of the poetic cycle Bauer found a con-
venient structure. It enabled him to harness the power of concise
presentation without the risk of becoming too narrow in scope and
relevance. It also encouraged the kind of variation that can prevent
the tedium which may arise from a tendency to rely on heavily styl-
ized structures of repetition and emphasis.

> *"Doch wie einen flammenden Kern trage ich in mir*
> *Zuneigung."*

A keen observer of the humanity around him, Bauer never
neglected to probe into his own mind and soul. As a result, a good
part of his mature poetry is autobiographical in nature, laying bare
the matrix of his values and ideals. In some of these poems, a pro-
vocative stance is present to suggest that a statement more aggres-
sive than pure self-expression is intended. These poems in fact
complement the critical poetry discussed in the preceding pages.
They counterbalance their negative impulse with the positive aim to
stir and stimulate, to offer example and guidance. The traces of such
an intent are, of course, found in most of Bauer's autobiographical
reflections. However, the present context allows inclusion of only

those poems in which offering this kind of direction is clearly the main concern.

The two cardinal virtues held up by these "exemplary" pieces are appreciation and affection. This is not immediately apparent in the short text titled "Für das köstliche Blau" (LL 86; KN 12), which seems to reject rather than express appreciation of things valued by people of sensitivity and culture. The speaker cites the splendours of nature ("das köstliche Blau des Himmels," line 1; "die keusche Schönheit des Winterschnees," line 4; "das ungeheure Flammen der Sonne," line 5). He cites the achievements of philosophy, knowledge, jurisprudence ("alle Philosophie, alle Bibliotheken, alle / Erörterungen der Menschenrechte," lines 7–8). He cites the sum total of religion and history ("die Kreuzigung Christi, ... alle Verbrennungen / von Ketzern," lines 10–11), and even human dignity ("sogar ... die / Unsterbliche Würde des Menschen," lines 14–15). All these, he insists, he will relinquish "Für einen Teller Suppe" (lines 3; 6; 9; 16). A wonderfully provocative piece, this list of renunciations throws into sharp relief what the readers, addressed emphatically as "Meine Damen und Herren" (line 13), are urged to consider: the wisdom to appreciate the basic materials, without which none of nature's offerings could be enjoyed and none of the manifold constructs of the human mind could exist – that which the affluent societies on both sides of the Atlantic consume or throw away without a thought.

Appreciation of such "luxuries," on which life is built, is the idea central to the poem "Paroles Essentielles" (LL 99–100). Mallarmé's well known words on words are borrowed and reinterpreted to point up Bauer's message: "rich" is the man who can afford all the necessities and some extra items on his shopping list of basics. These are:

Brot, Gemüse, Fleisch,
Zwiebeln, Tabak, Kaffee, Milch;
Auch Briefmarken ...
Auch eine Flasche Whisky ...
Auch die Zeitung
Auch die frische Wäsche ... (I: st. 1, lines 5–10)

The speaker's – we may safely say: Bauer's – appreciation of these "riches" stems from his own experience of poverty, and from the knowledge that it may return:

Es war nicht immer so.
Deshalb verstehe ich diese Worte.

Eines Tages mag es wieder anders sein.
Um so besser verstehe ich sie heute. (II: st. II)

His appreciation is nourished by affection: affection, first of all, for the hard-working providers of his childhood, here represented by his mother. The powerful image by which he remembers her shows her sitting at the kitchen table, carefully composing her shopping list "mit zerwaschener Hand mit einem Bleistiftstummel" (I: st. II, line 3), crossing out items that were too expensive, hence "Nicht für uns" (I: st. II, line 8). Affection also for those who today have nothing to eat and into whose "language" he takes the trouble to translate Mallarmé's words:

Paroles essentielles:
Mallarmé suchte nach ihnen.
Hier sind sie:
Brot, Milch, Fleisch. Übersetze sie
in die Sprache derer, die heute nicht satt werden. (II: st. I, lines 1–5)

Empathy with those who did not or do not have is here put forward as the heart of a more thoughtful appreciation of the things we tend to take for granted.

Not only things – people, too, deserve our conscious appreciation. This is what "Kein Unterschied mehr" (LL 124) is telling its reader through the speaker's "exemplary" story. All the men and women that have intersected his life – great or small, dead or living, far or close: Plato (line 3) or students (lines 8–9); the poet Tu Fu (lines 4–5) or the woman who does his laundry (lines 10–12); the insurgents of the twentieth of July (lines 6–7) or the woman who cleans his office (lines 13–14) – all these people receive his equal appreciation because not unlike the bowl of soup, "Sie alle machten es mir möglich, zu leben" (line 18).

Finally, the reflections formulated under the pithy first line, "Daß ich hier bin, ist gut" (LL 79), bring together the important facets, the origins, and the ramifications of that combination of appreciation and affection Bauer finds in himself and commends to his reader. He starts out by stating in beautifully simple and suggestive words his satisfaction with having emigrated, and his awareness of what he owes to the "here" that resulted from that move (line 1). Immediately, other people enter the scene of his reflection: those whose lesser fortune serves to enhance his appreciation of what he may now enjoy, and those who taught him such thoughtfulness in the first place. These latter are, of course, his parents whose "wortlose eindeutige Unterweisung" he acknowledges thankfully (lines 3–8). The former are the refugees ("Flüchtlinge") whose "lange Wanderung" has not brought them to a haven where there is bread to eat, a roof under which to sleep, and a room of one's own (lines 10–15). It may be apt to point out that "refugees, camps, long journey" (line 15), over and above the historical reality they refer to, have symbolic implications, signalling the human condition. This provides the connection to the autobiographical flashback that outlines in a few strokes the evolution of the speaker's deep-seated "affection" (line 21) and how it has shaped his perception of others and his approach to them. To the child receiving his parents' "unequivocal instruction," the first meaningful "word" was "friend" (lines 16–17); the enthusiasm of youth intensified this word to a "cry"/"shout" of "brother" (line 18); the experience of life in turn trimmed them down to being silent (line 19) but pregnant with affection:

> Als ich anfing zu sprechen, war mein erstes Wort:
> Freund.
> Als ich älter wurde, rief ich: Bruder. –
> Jetzt schweige ich.
> Doch wie einen flammenden Kern trage ich in mir
> Zuneigung. (lines 16–21)

Silence and affection now act conjointly to hold together the human world by prompting positive neighbourly deeds to give the lie to clever talk about the "decline of the world": "Sie widersteht, wovon viele so eilfertig reden, / Dem Untergang der Welt" (lines 22–3). Here we have *in nuce* Bauer's brand of humanism. It is neatly exemplified by the professor's attempt to open doors for his students ("Kein Unterschied mehr," LL 124 [lines 8–9]).

Bauer's concept offers nothing overwhelmingly new. He deserves credit, however, for the courage and consistency with which he advocated an ideal easily and often held in contempt for its utter simplicity. Simplicity is also the word that describes well the form in which the message is presented. The four poems in question, short as they are, employ the whole array of rhetorical devices Bauer has come to make his own. But there is nothing obtrusive about these. Absorbed by their function, they work hand in hand with the purposeful simplicity of diction to produce poetry that offers a pleasant first reading and grows on the reader as he or she engages in more detailed study.

CHAPTER SIX

Old Virtues Revisited

꙳ *"Unter der großen,*
gleichgültigen, alles wärmenden
Sonne ..."

Almost one-half of the poetry written by Bauer in Canada and selected for publication in *Lebenslauf* is autobiographical: the speaking "I" and even the distanced "he" of some of these poems clearly stand for the poet himself. A good part of this intensely personal poetry is gathered in cycles: "Im Innern der Stadt," "Verse von einer Universität," "Im Lesesaal," "Interview mit einem älteren Mann." As indicated earlier, the poetic cycle as crafted by the mature Bauer offers some very effective poetry.

"Im Innern der Stadt" (LL 82–5) is a model of significant simplicity. It comprises fourteen numbered stanzaic units which range in length from five to fifteen short lines. They record the thoughts that flow through the speaker's mind as he strolls through downtown Toronto. As a whole, the cycle gives voice to an experience of heightened existential awareness, brought on by the wanderer's reflections on himself and the surrounding scene.

The setting for this experience is effectively rendered by the image of the speaker walking through the city and finding himself at the core or nucleus of a wave:

Im Innern der Stadt, im Kern
Der Woge, deren Brausen ich sonst
Höre von meinem Fenster ... (I: lines 2–4)

It brings to mind graphically the juxtaposition of motion and the stillness of centre; of the centre receiving definition from the motion around it, while being itself the seat and source of concentrated power; of this centre moving along with the linear sweep of the entire body of motion. This latter implication is reinforced by the circular structure of the whole cycle that results from the repetition of the wave image at the very end:

Schlendere ich
Im Innern der Stadt
Im Kern der Woge. (xiv: lines 7–9)

All these are significant aspects of the speaker's situation. Being at the core of the wave of life that floods through the city, he receives "definition" in the form of a correction of the false sense of apartness and importance which he harbours in the sheltered security of his own room away from the larger sphere of life shared with others:

Da bin ich sicher, da
Denke ich wunder was von mir.
Im Inneren der Stadt werde ich
Berichtigt. (i: lines 5–8)

Here, he is reduced to the simple fact of just being there, devoid of any distinguishing feature that might lend him an externally recognizable identity: "Ich falle nicht auf; und doch / Bin ich da. Es ist gut so" (ii: lines 3–4).

This insight, and its concomitant full acceptance of undistinguished, bare "Da-Sein" now and here, is rendered imaginatively by the following piece. It likens his face to a leaf which, like all other leaves, is turned towards the sun:

Alle Gesichter
Hell in der Sonne, leuchtende Blätter,
…
So meines auch, unkenntlich, als trüge ich
Eine Maske, doch das
Bin ich, das ist alles,
Was ich erhielt, was ich bin
Jetzt und hier:
Der Sonne zugewandt: ein Blatt. (iii: lines 1–2; 4–9)

Acceptance becomes whole-hearted appreciation as he remembers the "promises" he received during a similar downtown stroll in "spring," realizing that these have indeed been fulfilled:

Und doch, als ich
Im Frühjahr hier ging,
Genauso unerkannt,
Versprachen Luft und Licht so viel.
Trat es ein? Die Versprechungen,

Wurden sie gehalten? – O ja:
Ich bin immer noch hier. (IV: lines 5–11)

The question of the meaning of such "being here," which is at this
point sparked off by the sight of gulls and the idea that they might
be writing "messages" into the sky, leads to the same conclusion: the
only – and amply sufficient – message to be received and to be con-
sidered is the plain statement "I am here":

Botschaften?
Keine. –
Und warum eine Botschaft?
Es genügt: ich bin hier. –
Das ist alles, was der Flug sagt.
Also doch eine Nachricht. (V: lines 10–15)

This "message" points to the importance of the self as the stable
centre that was first implied by the wave image at the beginning of
the cycle. The motion around this centre is now recognized as being
ephemeral and ultimately meaningless:

Doch wer erwartet Erschütterungen?
Nur die Zeitungen reden davon,
Und die Nachricht von heute ist morgen
Abfall. Alles wird sich beruhigen.
Es geschieht nichts. (VI: lines 3–7)

Thus the speaker, wondering in front of a flower shop for whom he
might buy a rose, decides that he should buy it for himself to cele-
brate his own life:

Um zu feiern, daß ich in solchen Zeiten
So lange überlebte, und das
Ohne mein Zutun. (IX: lines 6–8)

He has managed still to exist in spite of his time, through still exist-
ence. However, as the immediate repetition of the leaf–and–sun met-
aphor underscores, this existence is one like any other (X), and one
that was not attained without considerable sacrifice:

Ich habe
Für meine unbemerkte Anwesenheit
In dieser Stadt
Eine ganze Menge bezahlt. (XI: lines 1–4)

This is an obvious reference to the "name," present and future, that
Bauer gave up when venturing into the anonymity of exile. All the
more heart–warming to him is the shock of unexpected recognition,
rendered aptly by a graphic metaphor describing an unexpected
greeting ("Hello") as a "lucky feather" floating downward from the
sky (or heaven?):

> Unerwartet
> Sagt eine Stimme "Hello".
> …
> Eine goldene Glücksfeder
> Schwebt vom Himmel, ich fange sie auf.
> "Hello – Hello", sage ich. (xii: lines 1–2; 5–7)

Yet he is fully reconciled to his unnoticed presence under an indif-
ferent sun that neither makes nor keeps any promise:

> Unter der großen,
> Gleichgültigen, alles wärmenden
> Sonne,
> Unter der schönen Sonne,
> Die weder verspricht noch hält … (xiv: lines 1–5)

This image, found in the final piece of the cycle, stands out thanks
to an elaborately prepared contrast. The God of money, in spite of
receiving temples everywhere, cannot guarantee security: "Enorme
Sicherheit der Banken. / Enorme Kraft der Erdbeben" (vi: lines 1–2).
His places of worship, and the security they offer, spread "shadow"
one cannot hope to escape:

> Enorme Sicherheit der Banken,
> In deren Schatten ich gehe.
> Man geht immer in ihrem Schatten. (viii: lines 1–3)

While his followers will continue to build and to beg, he will not
answer everyone's prayer:

> Eine neue Bank wird gebaut, bald
> Kommen die Gläubigen
> Zum täglichen Gottesdienst;
> Nicht alle Gebete werden erhört. (xiii: lines 5–8)

In contrast, the sun gives evenhandedly to all – no promises, just
"warmth," to use or to squander.

This is where the importance of the individual self comes into play. The "old man" seen "sitting in the sun" may be an example of one who failed and fails to use well the gift and its attendant responsibility, which he, too, received and is still receiving:

Jede große Stadt fordert.
Wenn man nicht zahlt … siehst du dort
Den alten Mann in der Sonne sitzen?
Sei wach. (xi: lines 5–8)

While he rests, the speaker walks:

Unter der großen warmen Sonne
Schlendere ich
Im Innern der Stadt,
Im Kern der Woge. (xiv: lines 6–9)

Two different ways of using the gift. The dynamic one – an unhasty, at once inwardly focused and outwardly receptive progression – is clearly affirmed by the concluding return to the cycle's signature image.

> "Wissen
> Durchleuchtet von Poesie:
> Der wahre Lehrer."

Gathered under the title "Verse von einer Universität" (LL 114–19) are thirteen pieces of varying length and diverse structural organization which together sound Bauer's paean to learning. Based on his experience and observation as a university teacher, they bring together ideas fundamental to his whole intellectual and creative endeavour. Here is a summary.

Learning is a process that unites teacher and student in a never ending, difficult, but joyful venture (ii, iii, vii). Both learn, both teach (v). They study the insights and errors stored in libraries – meeting places of "continents" (x); they draw on the teachings given, through word and deed, by great minds as well as simple people, dead or living (vi); they are open to inspiration by art and nature (viii). Central to their endeavour is an awareness of the connectedness of life and learning. Through the study of life "pressed into words" (ii) an appreciation of the fullness and beauty of the world is fostered (viii), and also an appreciation of the fact that all this is a privilege predicated on favourable life circumstances (IX). The only legitimate but urgently needed word after Auschwitz is the humane word (XI) – the vehicle of knowledge infused with a sense of beauty and hope (XII). Its wellspring is the human heart which gives, which receives, whose pulse feeds and informs the unending pursuit (XIII).

It is obvious that Bauer's roots are firmly established in the intellectual and aesthetic soil of his native country, reaching back as far as German romanticism. One need only reread Friedrich Schlegel's "Athenäums-Fragment" to recognize the source of much of his thinking. This has implications for his poetic style, as the present cycle clearly demonstrates. Bauer uses symbols and images that are beautiful, albeit familiar. Take, for example, the heart, "Der Quell, von dem du trinkst" (XIII: line 10); or the hand, "Die sich empor-streckt / Wie ein grüner Zweig" (I: lines 5–7); or the "hungry" eyes, "die der Suche nicht müde werden" (III: st.II, lines 1–2); or the flight of doves and clouds and thoughts over the green land and away from the frail body (IV); or the masters who have coined words, "Weil Leben in ihnen floß und rauschte" (II: lines 4–5); or indeed the notion and the words, "Wissen, / Durchleuchtet von Poesie" (XII: lines 1–2). These and other very effective images and expressions are found in all parts of the cycle. They may charm some of Bauer's readers, but do they appeal to a wider readership accustomed to the different sounds and images of the contemporary poetic scene?

The same question mark does not hang over the companion piece "Im Lesesaal" (LL 120–3). It is spoken with Bauer's own voice; sincere, largely straightforward, well tempered, and vivid. It combines atmospheric observation, description of significant moments in the learning process of young students, and reflection on his own learning, teaching, and writing.

The introductory piece sets the scene. Its subject is the charged silence that fills the reading room of a university library. Just scratch it with your fingernail, the second stanza suggests, and it will open and offer up what it holds:

Ritze sie
Nur mir dem Nagel des Fingers,
Und sie öffnet sich
Zur Verwirrung der Sprachen von Babel
Oder zur Ordnung der Welt. (I: st.II)

The two possible yields of this silence are, of course, mental processes, namely, the confusion or the clarification that may result from intense study, triggered at any moment by the slightest impulse. What makes this little poem so remarkable in the context of Bauer's poetry, is the fact that it keeps its metaphor intact and presents in seamless fusion concrete and abstract imagery and suggestion. No "wie"-comparison is given, the reading room *is* a container filled with silence:

> Der Lesesaal
> In der Bibliothek der Universität
> Ein Behälter, gefüllt mit Stille ... (I: st. I, lines 1–3)

The absence of the copula "ist" serves to veil, not to destroy this identification. And how do you scratch silence, causing it to open up, unless it has a hard surface? And where do the chaos or order come from? No explanation is offered, the reader must work it out both intellectually and imaginatively.

The second poem is appealing for quite a different reason. It describes, in vivid detail, "die Geburt eines Gedankens" (II: st. I, line 4). The introductory question, "Have you ever seen how a thought is born?" (II: st. I, lines 1–2) immediately sets the scene with an eye witness eager to share his experience of the "incomparably moving" event (line 5) he has seen. Thus the fictitious listeners' and the actual readers' interest has been secured. Describing in sequential detail the gestures involved, the speaker makes a fascinating drama of a young woman's struggle to wait out the gestation of her thought: first she fixed her gaze on nothing in front of her, then she ran her finger over her lips, her hand through her hair, she stared blankly into space, at her slightly raised left hand as if waiting for something to settle there (II: st. II). – Which actually happened:

> Es kam.
> Er kam: Der Gedanke.
> Er kam: ein seltner glänzender Vogel ... (II: st.III, lines 1–3)

This dramatic climax is effectively structured to mark the important moment, and to build up renewed curiosity for the "moving" things that happened next. At this point, imagination takes over, describing in dramatic detail how this little phoenix came flying across the hall, settled on her slightly raised finger, hopped onto her shoulder and sang into her ear. With a laconic "Sie schrieb," structured to parallel the central turning point, the narrator ends this captivating account.

In another, no less engaging piece, the older reading-room observer is taken by a smile which he catches on the face of a young man absorbed in his reading. The observer interprets the smile as the reader's return gift for the smile he has just found in the pages – hidden there centuries ago by a "distant friend":

> Wem lächelte er zu?
> Einem fernen Freunde,
> Der, vor Jahrhunderten gestorben,
> In seinem Logbuch
> Ein Lächeln versteckt hatte,
> Und er fand es.
> …
> Und gab es zurück. (v: lines 3–8; 12)

Clearly, this impressionistic scene, whether an account of something that actually happened or a product of the poet's imagination, serves as a vehicle for his own hope for an appreciative reception of what he himself has taken pains to "hide" in his "log book."

I come now to the "confessional" part of the cycle, in which Bauer takes a public look at himself as a teacher (IV), as a writer (VI), as the student that he never ceased to be (VII). These intensely personal reflections do, however, transcend the merely personal. While formulating ideas and perceptions fundamental to Bauer's thinking, they offer valuable food for thought to anyone who cares to read, write, or teach. They are written in smoothly flowing free verse and are free of heavy rhetoric or emotion.

The poem dealing with Bauer, the teacher, starts with an apparently self-critical assessment whose ironical undercurrent is soon recognized. He states simply and plainly that he has been "ein mittelmäßiger Lehrer" (IV: st. 1, line 1), an average or even mediocre teacher because – unlike scholars in his field – he was unable to categorize, and lacked ultimate answers and judgments (IV: st. 1, lines 2–5). He has not dedicated all his life to acquiring or "collecting" knowledge (lines 6–7), and his response to literature is to its human dimension, not to the letter:

> Zudem dachte ich zu oft
> An Schweiß, Agonie, zu mißliche Umstände derer,
> Die Bücher schrieben, Stücke, und Verse,
> Aufschreie von Lebenden hörte ich zu oft
> In ihren Logbüchern. (IV: st. 1, lines 8–12)

An apparent apology, these reflections do in fact add up to the humanist's affirmation of his different approach. His teaching was "mittelmäßig" by the standards that he thereby rejects.

Consistently, he now proceeds to expand on his own vision and practice. To throw the contrast into sharp relief, he begins with a positive statement about his quality as a teacher that parallels its critical counterpart in the preceding stanza: "Ich war ein guter Lehrer, wie ich hoffe" (st. II, line 1). He hopes to have been a good teacher, as he "tried to open doors." One notes the juxtaposition of ("Methode and Sammlung des Wissens" (st. I, lines 2 and 7) with "ich versuchte Türen zu öffnen" (st. II, line 2). It serves to bring out the contrast between knowing how to collect and confine in categories abstract subject-matter, and making an effort to mediate the widening of horizons for human beings. As a people-oriented teacher he is quick to acknowledge the helpful instruction he has received from people: from the "silent ones," such as his shoemaker, to the "powerful speakers," the masters of the mind:

> Denen ich Belehrung verdankte,
> Eingeschlossen mein ukrainischer Schuhmacher
> Wie meine Freunde,
> Eingeschlossen die Flüchtlinge von überall
> Wie die Meister,
> Die Stummen eingeschlossen wie die Wortmächtigen. (IV: st. II, lines 4–9)

His school of people does not recognize any teacher/student hierarchy. The only difference between the two parties to the learning process is the greater vulnerability of those who have been exposed to life's hard knocks for a longer period of time:

> ... der Unterschied war,
> Daß ich, bei längerem Leben, mehr Narben trug,
> Und zuweilen, auch im Lehren,
> Brachen sie auf. (IV: st. III, lines 2–5)

The voice of Bauer, the writer, sounds less assertive. Understandably so, because he does not measure himself against peers whose ideas and methods he rejects, but against masters whose works he admires. His encounter with them, he confesses, has sometimes led to paralysing embarrassment and shock:

> O so überwältigend hoffnungslos
> Erschien mir da mein Versuch.

O so langsam war mir meine Hand,
Und im Rauschen des Stromes
Entschwand mir der Ton meiner Quelle. (vi: lines 6–10)

What lifted him up from such dejection was the thought that he, the living author, still had a chance:

Noch immer war ich
Der Suchende,
Andiamo, wir sind unterwegs:
Klopfte mein Herz. (vi: lines 13–16)

Bauer, the elderly student with many scars, freely admits to his yearning for the freshness of a first intellectual encounter – only to retract this statement and assure his reader, or himself, that in spite of his years, his joy of learning is as fresh as ever:

Gern möchte ich den frischen Geschmack
Des Honigs aus unzähligen Waben
Zum ersten Mal im Munde spüren;
...
Auch mir, einem älteren Mann,
Schmeckt der Honig
Immer noch gut, noch immer frisch. (vii: lines 2–4; 6–8)

This mixed message serves nicely to convey a sense of wisdom tempered with nostalgia, which lends a very human face to the "elderly man" who draws inspiration not only from books but also from the sight of young people "im Lesesaal." The reader is reminded of this locale by the imagery employed, quite aptly, to conclude the emotionally charged poetic "record" there conceived and thus titled. A honey image was used in the middle of the cycle: the shelves filled with books were likened to hives in which the students search for honey:

Zu den vollen Bücherregalen
Treten sie, junge Männer und Mädchen und ältere,
Wie zu Bienenstöcken.
Schweigend suchen sie nach Honig. (iii)

This comparison prepares the metaphor at the end: I may be an elderly man (who in the course of his life has eaten a lot of honey), but the taste of honey is still good, still fresh to me. Such poetically expressive advocacy of incessant study and search to foster growth and development throughout one's life betrays the experienced hand of the "elderly" poet.

⚡ *"Ich liebe Menschen"*

The relatively lengthy "Interview mit einem älteren Mann" (LL 131–8; eighteen pieces of varying length) is a self-portrait and as such an important part of Bauer's entire poetic "Bericht." There can be no doubt that behind the "elderly man" stands the poet himself, and that he wanted his reader to know it. In section IX, for example, the man who is being interviewed identifies himself unmistakably as Walter Bauer by giving verifiable personal information:

Daß ich hier liege
In einem Bett, das nicht mir gehört,
In der Roxborough Street East
In Toronto ... (IX: lines 16–19)

In fact, whatever the "elderly man" says in the course of the "Interview" points to the man who created him to give a summation of himself – for the "record."

This self-presentation is cast in the form of a reported interview which provides a serviceable structure for the rendering of distanced subjectivity. The three voices identifiable in the setting are first, an eye witness who is giving his detached, accurate account of a question-and-answer session held by a group of people and a man; secondly, this group, variously referred to as "man" or "sie"; and thirdly, a man, referred to as "er." The scene is set at the beginning:

Als man ihn fragte,
Wen er am meisten geliebt habe,
Schwieg er, aber sie konnten sehen,
Daß ... (I: st. I, lines 1–4)

"Schweig und verrate niemand",
Sagte er dann, "das las ich ..." (I: st. II, lines 1–2)

The narrator's account is rendered in the past indicative: "when they asked him /... / he said nothing, but they could see ..." (st. I, lines 1, 3–4). All questions are cited in the subjunctive of indirect speech without any further explanation or comment: "wen er ... geliebt habe" (st. I, line 2). All answers, with one exception, are given in quotation marks (" ... "), sometimes commented on or explicitly marked out as the man's response.

Such faithful differentiation determines the structure of the entire "Interview." However, the dominant pattern is broken four times in differing degrees of subtlety or conspicuousness. In these passages, the dividing lines between the voices of the "reporter" and the "elderly man" are blurred and the two identities seem to merge.

In section VII, the initial question is followed by an unmarked comment which is neither the man's direct answer nor one of the narrator's usual interjections (he said, he added, etc.):

Er hatte allerlei verloren, denn in
Solchen Zeiten hatte er gelebt.
Ein ganzes Heft hätte er
Vollschreiben können, betitelt:
Verluste. (VII: lines 4–8)

He had lost enough to fill volumes titled "Losses." This could well be the man's mental response to the question just posed: whether losses could still affect him ("Ob Verluste / Ihn noch treffen könnten / Und welche?" lines 1–3). It could also be a comment made by the narrator who thereby betrays knowledge of the man and his life.

Later on in his report the narrator actually takes it upon himself to relate the legend with which the man explained his position on God. Curiously, the account of the other's narration slips imperceptibly into the direct narrative mode. Here is the relevant passage:

Da erzählte er ihnen
Die alte jüdische Legende von dem Rabbi
In einem kleinen Dorf in Polen, der nachts
In die Synagoge ging, seine Runde machend wie üblich,
Und der in einer dunklen Ecke
Gott sitzen sah.
Da fiel er nieder auf sein Gesicht und rief:
"Herr, was tust du hier? Und Gott antwortete ihm,
Nicht in Donner und Sturm, sondern
Mit leiser Stimme:
"Ich bin müde, Rabbi, ich bin sterbensmüde." (Interview," XI: line 3–13)

This narration is followed, with no guidance other than the subjunctive form of the verb, by a question put to the original narrator, the man interviewed: "Was das mit ihm zu tun habe?" (line 14). His concluding response is cited, as usual, in quotation marks: "'Ich will ihn nicht noch müder machen. / Er hat genug zu tragen.'" (XI: lines 15–16).

Following such subtle (con-)fusion is a passage that seems designed to make it just a little more transparent. Visible markers are given to signal the critical moment:

Ob er denn
Ein Volk besonders liebe?
(Und er sah in ihren Augen eine Fahne, aber
Er konnte nicht sehen, von welcher Farbe.)
"Ich liebe Menschen", sagte er. (xii: lines 1–5)

The brackets point to the narrator, telling us that the man, when asked whether he harboured any special love of a particular people (lines 1–2), could see a flag in the eyes of his questioners, without, however, being able to determine its colour. The way in which this piece of information is integrated into the flow of the interview suggests that during its progress the narrator is privy to what is going on the man's mind.

At the end of the "Interview," the two identities finally merge. The man is invited to formulate a message to his friends, both known and unknown (xviii: lines 1–3). He obliges with a quotation from St. John Perse, which he then (lines 6–7) renders in German:

"S'en aller! S'en aller!
Parole de vivant!"
Vorwärts!
Das Wort des Lebenden! (xviii: lines 4–7)

Or so it seems. The established pattern of presentation would make the French words his own, and their German version the narrator's concluding comment.

The narrator, then, flag in hand, is playing a game of hide-and-seek, creating his double to mobilize the combined forces of detached accuracy and personal authority. And, as the ostensible self-quotation indicates, he is doing it *in loco auctoris.*

With this "Interview" the poet Bauer presents the man whose thought and sensibility informs his creative endeavour, whose principal aim is not to give aesthetic pleasure but to make a humanistic statement, fashioned to appeal to the reader's ethical conscience. This could not sit too well with his intended readers, the older ones preferring to "forget," the younger ones to discuss existential *angst.* Bauer, of course, was aware of the distance that separated him from his time. Politely, he reduced it to a bridgeable gap between generations. The attribute "elderly," apart from its biographical accuracy, seems chosen to stress the life experience that bestows wisdom and authority and legitimizes the "elderly man's" sense of superiority. Referring to the young people who are said to "condemn" the old, he comments: "'Sie haben es schwer, jung zu sein, / Und sie werden auch älter, wie ich hoffe'" (VI: lines 5–6). Growing older no doubt is to say growing wiser and, as he elaborates, breaking out of the prisons in which they allow themselves to be held (line 10). To achieve freedom from the ideas that are currently holding them captive, they will have to embrace what they consider old-fashioned: "'Ohne die alten Tugenden / Werden auch sie nicht auskommen'" (VI: lines 11–12). Advocacy of "the old virtues" was one of Bauer's central concerns. To give the advocate a distinct face and voice, he has created the fictitious interview with him.

He is a man of flesh and blood who has had his share of disappointments: "'Ich habe Aphrodite geliebt, / Aber sie antwortete nicht'" (II: lines 7–8). While lifting the veil this much, the speaker rejects firmly any further intrusion into his private domain. The question whom he had loved most (I: st. 1, line 2) is met first with silence and then with a citation of some lines about appropriate silence, which he had read in his youth before ever being in love:

"Schweig und verrate niemand",
Sagte er dann, "das las ich
In einem Roman meiner Jugend
Als ich noch nicht liebte." (I: st. 11)

He thus stamps this kind of information as irrelevant to the portrait for which he is sitting.

Asked about any other "loves," he cites "Blumen ... und Blüten" for the greeting they extend silently when it is needed most: "'Vor allem die ersten Blüten / Nach dem Winter, der nicht nur / Alternden Leuten schwerfällt'" (III: lines 9–11). What matters more than the beauty of flowers is their silent but friendly existence: "'Sie schweigen. Sie blühen,'" (III: line 4). This is both image and model to the humanist whose heart goes out to "the human being," without whom he would see no purpose in being: "'Was sollte ich hier ohne ihn?'" (IV: line 3). Importantly, loving the species does not mean loving every specimen: "Hinzufügend: "'Gewissen Zeitgenossen / Gehe ich aus dem Wege,'" (IV: lines 4–5). Firm convictions bring with them firm associations and firm dissociations – the latter to the point of implacable hatred:

Ob er denn auch hasse? –
"Ja."

Ob er sich mit jedem versöhnen könnte? –
"Nein." (viii: lines 1–4)

Significantly, this "hatred"results in avoidance, not confrontation. The "contemporaries" Bauer preferred to avoid (iv: lines 4–5) were, more than any other, fellow Germans – members of the politically engaged literary guild in Germany and those who had emigrated to seek their fortune in Canada. Two relevant diary entries will serve to illustrate this: "Their good intentions make for pitiful literature. Their hysteria is frightening. Should I have a part in it? Should I allow myself to be contaminated by it? *This* solidarity is a weak thing ... I am an alien and I can and must draw riches from my alienness. – To this day I am dismayed at their mental poverty and hysteria. Germans will get *personal*" (May 1, 1958).[1] A visit to the German Club in Kitchener prompted this comment: "It was horrifying ... *Why is it so difficult to be in the company of Germans* – this kind of Germans. Between Parzifal and goose step there is nothing for these Germans ... no humanity. This indescribable clumsiness. This rivalry into which I, a stranger, was drawn immediately. This mixture of helplessness, arrogance and dishonesty. This lack of form" (May 12, 1958)[2]

Returning to the poetic "Interview" – to counterbalance the negativity of his admission of aversion and hatred, the speaker finds an opportunity to repeat emphatically the important part of his statement: "'Ich liebe Menschen'" (xii: lines 5; 10). And at the end we learn that this love of human beings inspires him not with mere hope, but with total confidence:

So habe er
Für den Menschen
Tatsächlich Hoffnung! –
"Nicht Hoffnung.
Gewißheit." (xvi: lines 6–10)

Spaced strategically over the entire "Interview," "Ich liebe Menschen" appears to be its principal message. The passages in between draw the various significant lines that characterize the face of the man who is making this confession.

Bauer's political affiliation, symbolized by colour preference, was once "red" (v: lines 9–10) – one remembers his Leuna-poetry; now his favoured colour is "white," the colour of all-uniting oneness and total openness and commitment to the future:

"Weiß", antwortete er,
"Das alle Farben enthält;

Und weiß ist die Fläche,
Auf die Zukunft
Geschrieben werden kann." (v: lines 4–8)

He then adds "blue." As he indicated earlier, this colour – the colour
of romantic yearning – to him spells friendliness extended by one
being to another:

"Auch Blau möchte ich nennen,
Es ist die Farbe
Der afrikanischen Veilchen
Auf meinem Fensterbrett,
Die Farbe eines zarten Saluts
Der mich oft und beglückend
Unerwartet traf." (v: lines 12–18)

Having lived in troubled times, the losses that could still affect him
would be the loss of his eyes, his heart, and his laughter:

"Der Verlust der Augen,
Um das Licht zu sehen.
Der Verlust des Herzens,
Um noch bewegt zu werden.
Der Verlust des Lachens." (vII: lines 9–13)

Again the voice of the man who loves human beings is heard, of the
man who dearly desires friendly contact with them. His deepest con-
cerns, indicated by the thoughts that fill his sleepless nights, centre
on people: parents, siblings, friends, his future readers, referred to as
friends (IX: lines 6–15). He is haunted by the uncertainty of seeing
another tomorrow, undoubtedly because of the opportunity that
might be lost to transform into deed the dictates of his mind and
heart (IX: lines 3–5). He is moved by the "overwhelming" and well
appreciated fact of "being here," under the specific circumstances of
his life, occupying a specific place in a world immensely larger than
himself:

"Daß ich hier liege
In einem Bett, das nicht mir gehört,
In der Roxborough Street East
In Toronto
In Kanada
Auf dem amerikanischen Kontinent
In der Welt

Unter dem Himmel, der alles umspannt,
Ziemlich unverständlich, doch
Überwältigend.
Daß ich hier bin, und das
Ist noch immer sehr gut." (ix: lines 16–27)

As one might expect, his regrets have to do with personal failure
both in the private sphere and on the wider sociopolitical scene. The
list of regrets is revealing:

Ob er etwas bedaure? –
"Ja. Viele Menschen
Tiefer verletzt zu haben, als ich wollte."
"Feige gewesen zu sein,
Wenn ich hätte mutig sein sollen."
"Überlebt zu haben,
Wenn so viele starben und soviel Bessere."
"Vor Furcht gezittert zu haben,
Wenn ich hätte furchtlos sein sollen."
"Gekrochen zu sein,
Wenn ich hätte aufrecht gehen sollen."
"Daß mein Schatten
Mir oft schwer wurde, da ich
Ein Deutscher zu meinen Zeiten war."
"Nicht Besseres getan zu haben.
Nicht froher gewesen zu sein.
Nicht großherziger.
Ja: nich großherziger. Es ist davon
Zuwenig in der Welt.
Nun, ich lebe noch. Ich lerne noch." (xiii: lines 1–20)

Typically, this litany of regrets ends on an upbeat note that affirms
this man's unbending will to "learn" and do better in the future.

He is no stranger to "Melancholie," but his positive spirit pre-
vails and enables him to appreciate it as "the salt on his bread"
and a counterweight that brings out more clearly "the good
things": "'Die guten Dinge erhalten durch sie / Mehr Licht'" (x:
lines 7–8). Religion does not feature in his scheme of the world.
The legend of the Jewish rabbi, quoted earlier (p. 96), serves to
explain his position of considerate distance that neither detracts
nor ridicules (xi).

Free from any political or religious ties, he remains firmly attached
both to his "unfortunate" people and to his own Germanness:

"Ja", fügte er hinzu, "ich liebe
Mein unglückliches Volk, je unglücklicher
Es wird in seinem satten Glück, um so mehr
Hänge ich an ihm ..."
...
"Ich werde noch am letzten Tage
Aus deutschem Lehm gemacht worden sein." (xii, lines 6–9; 15–16)

The language he shares with his fellow Germans is the object of his deepest love. His response to the relevant question is a judiciously controlled emotional torrent that displays the whole spectrum of the intensely somatic, emotional, intellectual, historical, cultural, and political dimensions of his intimate bond with the language of his origin. A sensitive chord has been struck and the poet (cum rhetorician) responds with the power of expression that this language has put at his disposal. A few excerpted lines will suffice to illustrate this:

"Die Sprache der Quellen tief in mir
In der Erde von Jahrtausenden.
...
Die Sprache, die in mir fließt wie mein Blut,
Atmet, lacht, klagt,
Die zu meinen Zeiten geschunden wurde.
Die Sprache, in der das Wasser des kleinen Flusses rann.
Die Sprache, in der die ersten Frühlinge kamen.
Die Sprache, in der die Männer des zwanzigsten Juli
Neunzehnhundertvierundvierzig
Die Würde des Menschen verteidigten." (xiv: lines 4–5; 9–16)

The same power of expression serves him to pay some genuine compliments to the language of his later and last years:

"Die Sprache, die mich als Gast empfing und reich bewirtete,
...
Die Sprache, die mir großzügig erlaubte,
In ihr zu Hause zu sein
Als Gast, als Emigrant, als Freund der Welt." (xiv: lines 21; 25–7)

The last line calls to mind Bauer's self-description as "ein Deutscher in der Welt." As a German citizen of the world he does not feel uprooted. His human roots reach deep into the "earth," wherever in the world he happens to be:

"Sind meine Wurzeln
Nicht in der Erde dort,
Wo ich bin?
Meine Wurzeln sind
In der Erde." (xv: lines 3–7)

His concluding summation reiterates two familiar and clearly central Bauer themes. First, full acceptance of his own life: "'Ich war hier,/ Es war gut, hier zu sein'" (xvii: lines 10–11). Secondly, hope-inspired untiring endeavour to use life well:

"S'en aller! S'en aller!
Parole de vivant!"
Vorwärts!
Das Wort des Lebenden! (xviii: lines 4–7)

The portrait of the man who advocates "the old virtues" clearly serves as a vehicle to present them in palatable form. These "virtues" and their presentation through a living exemplar are indeed of venerable age, at least as old as Lessings *Nathan der Weise*. Bauer is portraying his own verifiable experience to breathe fresh life into these ideas and to impress on reluctant contemporaries their continued relevance. The indifference meted out to Bauer's work indicates that his contemporaries were not impressed by the universal message sent out to them.

CHAPTER SEVEN

Theatrum Mundi

"Dämonen zeitlos in der Zeit."

A writer who insists that his poetry is neither to serve a social or political agenda, nor to convey a "message" or "moral," would severely undermine his credibility if he confined his observation and reflection to the contemporary scene and offered nothing more far-reaching than the specific social criticism and corrective conceptual model that have been discussed in the two preceding chapters. It is therefore important to realize that the potentially compromising specificity of Bauer's social criticism and advice is thoroughly embedded in the universal perspective that informs all of his thinking and writing. He does take aim at the materialism and complacency of his contemporaries, both in North America and Europe, but he perceives and presents these traits as a manifestation of human nature typical of the given place and time. By carefully mixing specific and universal reflections he keeps alive the reader's awareness of the relevance of both and avoids the Scylla of narrowness and the Charybdis of abstraction. The entire body of Canadian poetry included in *Lebenslauf* constitutes such a strategic mix, from the deceptively unassuming specificity of the short poem "Eine Grenze" (LL 80) to the sweeping universality of "Bruegel: Die Blinden" (LL 139–41). The co-presence and equal validity of these two complementary dimensions of Bauer's thought and work should be carefully borne in mind, even though critical discussion must deal with them in succession. This chapter, then, will take a closer look at those poems in which the universal sounds of the age-old *vanitas*-plaint are intoned, complete with Bauer's own *carpe diem.*

The "mortality" of cities, impressive products of human culture, is the idea central to the expansive Whitmanesque piece "Ich habe Rom gesehn zu manchen Zeiten" (LL 111–12; KN 65–66). The bulk of the poem is made up of the speaker's account of his visits to important cultural centres such as Rome, London, and New York, and his sensitive appreciation of their sights and cultural-historical riches (lines 1–32). The sharp profile and the communicative immediacy of a postscript combine to voice his saddened dismay about the fact that cities may be erased in a flash, that people have in the past destroyed – and may do the same in the future – the magnificent monuments to their own greatness:

PS.
Doch wollt ihr wissen, warum Tränen mir im Auge waren,
Als ich New York, die Stadt der Städte, sah?
Daß Städte sterben können, haben wir erfahren.
Ein Feuerfall, ein Flammenwind. Nichts war mehr da. (Lines 33–6)

The short poem "Eine Grenze" (LL 80; NT 43) continues and expands the theme of human destructiveness. The speaker tells of a painful division of his heart, caused by the partition of his "old country," and a contingent agonized yearning for the wholeness that has been lost. The political situation of the day, Germany cut in two, acts as a depressing reminder of what is at work in the making of history – blindness in the guise of wisdom:

Blindheit, die sich für Weisheit ausgab,
Versuchte, Geschichte zu machen –
So machten sie immer Geschichte. (Lines 3–5)

The blindness of those responsible for the division of this particular country at this particular time in history is but a phenotypic variant of the blindness that (mis)guides all players in the historical arena. Such "Geschichtspessimismus" is apt to blunt any political will and to invite the resigned retroversion at the end of the poem: "Heute nacht sehne ich mich zurück / nach dem Ganzen" (lines 13–14). Needless to say, in this Bauer is not alone. The sentiment and attitude here expressed have haunted and paralysed countless fellow Germans since the days of the romantic movement.

Following immediately is the equally short and thought-provoking piece "Teller reinigend von Überresten" (LL 81; NT 42). Reaching back to the cradle of Western thought, it considers, in Socratic fashion, "Wieviel in der Welt / Zu den Überresten gehört" (lines 12–13): how much in this – as we know: blind – world is leftover, remainder, waste; how much should be discarded because it has lost its value and usefulness, or how much is left to waste because its value and usefulness are not appreciated. The autobiographical dimension of this poem favours the second reading. The anomalous situation of an educated dishwasher on night shift sets the scene for undisturbed reflection about the self in its present sorry circumstances, and about the world at large with its perennially sorry state of affairs:

Teller reinigend von den Überresten,
Denke ich nach.
…
Ungestört wandern meine Gedanken
Hierhin und dorthin und kommen zurück.
Und ich denke nach,
Ein nächtlicher Schüler Sokrates',
Fragen stellend. (Lines 1–2; 5–9)

Withholding his answer, the speaker guides his reader in the direction of a less than uplifting conclusion: may the reader verify for himself or herself that the world is – has always been – brimming with waste.

Worse still, the insensitivity, misjudgment, and even crime that have created such "Überreste" are conveniently aided and abetted by such powerful allies as the passage of time and the way in which historical fact is commonly transmitted and evaluated. Under the title "Geschichtsbücher oder: die Zeit vergeht" (LL 113) one reads:

Die Schuld stirbt aus
Mit den Schuldigen und Schuldlosen,
…
Die Söhne erinnern sich noch, aber
Es bewegt sie nicht mehr.
Die Enkel lesen davon noch in Geschichtsbüchern.
…
Der Schrecken schrumpft zu ein paar Zeilen zusammen,
Die Hinrichtungen werden zusammengefaßt als: beträchtlich.
Die Geschichtsschreiber verteilen die Zensuren je nach Standpunkt.
(Lines 1–2; 8–10; 14–16)

The horror is reduced to a few lines, executions are summarized as "considerable" (lines 14–15). What once affected living beings, in time becomes paper knowledge available at leisure, cigarette in hand. Any questioning that may occur in the course of its acquisition will at best amount to a brief flaring up of inconsequential curiosity:

Die riesigen Rauchwolken über den Lagern
Werden zum leichten Aschefleck auf weißem Papier,
Leicht weggeblasen, oder zur stummen Frage des Lesenden:
So viele? Wie machte man das? – und er liest weiter. (Lines 17–20)

A real lesson, one that translates into attitude and action, will never be learned:

Die Belehrungen, die wie
Worte des Jüngsten Gerichts hätten hallen sollen,
Werden nie mehr gehört. (Lines 21–3)

Driving home the point in graphic detail, the poetic portrait "Goya: Haus des Tauben" (LL 128–30) culminates in this unsettling picture of the human world:

"Ich hab gesehn." Sein Testament: Nichts wird gelernt.
Ein Schmatzen, Schlürfen, Rülpsen Tag und Nacht im Haus.
Saturn zerfleischt sein Kind. (St. IV, lines 15–17)

Nothing is ever learned in this world in which mankind engages in self-slaughter. These are strong words and images emanating from the pen of gentle Walter Bauer. The portrait of an artist larger than himself, who lived his life fully and wisely, who observed his time and left his "record," serves to convey and authenticate the disturbing knowledge of the harm wrought by ever active "Dämonen zeitlos in der Zeit" (st. IV, line 13). In his Goya essay, "Das Lichte und das Dunkle" (1940), Bauer had written: "A man of the eighteenth century ... tears open the bottom of life; everything gushes forth, except beauty and love. The demons of avarice, stupidity, greed of all kinds seize power. What comes to life in this work is no longer the eighteenth century ... It is *the* world, – the world of all times."[1]

In the context of his poem, Bauer invokes a variety of cultural periods, separated by time and space, to underscore the universality of the observed truth: a Spanish artist of the enlightened eighteenth and early nineteenth century, mixing the ingredients of classical antiquity ("Saturn" [st. IV, line 8]; "Koloß" [line 9]; "Parzen" [line 12]), Christian mythology ("San Isidoro," "Pilger" [line 10]), and medieval superstition ("Hexe" [line 12]); all this contemplated and borrowed creatively in the middle of the scientific twentieth century by a German poet in North America.

One of the greatest "recording" agents of the human circus was Pieter Bruegel. It comes as no surprise that this old master features prominently in Bauer's selected anthology. The piece in question, "Bruegel: Die Blinden" (LL 139–41), occupies pride of place at the very end of *Lebenslauf*, offering, as it were, the poet's "last word," recorded "at the end, not the beginning": "So letzte Worte werden / Am Ende, nicht am Anfang, aufgezeichnet und signiert" (st. 1, lines 5–6). Significantly, these concluding words lack the pungency of those hurled at the reader in the Goya portrait. The reason for this is clear. While the Goya poem takes aim at undesirable facets of human nature and behaviour, the Bruegel poem depicts the human condition – "die Situation des Menschen in der Welt," as Bauer confirms in his Bruegel essay, "Die Weisheit der Tiefe" (*Die zweite Erschaffung der Welt* 29). What could conceivably be corrected or modified draws harsh criticism; what is beyond man's control is sympathetically recorded.

The poem begins with a brief description of the scene depicted in Bruegel's painting "The Blind Leading the Blind" (st. I, lines 1–5). This painting, the reader is told, is the "testament" (line 5) of one who lived and worked shoulder to shoulder with other "visionaries" in a time of profound change:

… Genosse in der Zeit
Von Rabelais, Montaigne, Shakespeare: Sehenden. So er.
Die Zeit knirscht zwischen Alt und Neu unübersichtlich
Und will, in Furcht und Hunger, Unbekanntes. – (St. 1, lines 7–10)

The importance of such a man's "last words" being obvious, the speaker draws special attention to the fact that they are different from the rest of his work:

Doch vor dem Bettlerbild ist anderes:
Der ganze Bruegel und sein Inventar in Flandern:
In der Welt." (St. 1, lines 11–13)

The "Bettlerbild" brings something new, and herein lies its particular significance.

The second stanza sums up, in thirty-one lines, the "entire Bruegel" that precedes this final statement – his fascinating pandemonium of the human world, endowed with Flemish faces and set in a Flemish landscape: the fall of Icarus that goes unnoticed (lines 1–2); the Tower of Babel that was never to be (lines 3–4); the Crucifixion that looks like a "Volksfest" unconcerned about the person of the crucified (lines 5–6); the infanticide instigated by Herod and the census undertaken by Augustus (line 7); the seasons of the year depicted in contemporary rural scenes (lines 11–16); dancing, carousing, gluttony, excess, greed, war (lines 17–28) – and ultimately the "black triumph" of Death, who levels all to "waste, carrion, putrefaction" ("Abfall, Aas, Verwesung," line 29). The sum total: human life, the way it is lived, boils down to vain folly and mindless conformity:

> … Alles ist Narrheit, alles eitel, weil
> Alles Leben ist, Spiel wie von Kindern, ernsthaft, ohne Lachen,
> Sprichwörter, denen jeder folgt, obgleich er sie durchschaut;
> Durchschauen hilft nicht, mitgefangen, mitgehangen. (St. II, lines 21–4)

This, not unlike Goya's gallery, is a sobering account indeed. However, as the present poem insists, it does not give us the Old Master's "last words." These were rendered in the old image of the blind leading the blind. It is a far cry from the blunt cynicism of Goya's "testament" and the critical realism of Bruegel's earlier work. While demonstrating the "fall" that is inevitably brought about by human "blindness," both this condition and its consequence are depicted in a manner which bespeaks empathy and which offers reassurance that the inevitable is not the end.

The universal application of this image is spelled out clearly by the commentator: "Da kommen sie, sechs Bettler, blind, ein Augenloser führt sie./ So jeden Tag; so diesen" (st. III, lines 4–5). The attendant didactic impetus, too, is deliberately exploited. But rather than pointing a critical finger at these blind fools, this poem focuses on the fellowship that binds them, the sense of security and warmth they derive from their experience of interdependence and mutual trust which their shared handicap imposes on them:

> … Ihm [dem ersten] vertraun sie blindlings;
> So auch vertrauen sie einander, und die Hand,
> Die sie auf Vordermannes ungesehne Schulter legen,
> Gefühlt, doch nie erblickt, bindet zu Sicherheit und Wärme.
>
> (St. III, lines 5–8)

Such empathetic observation is the new feature that Bauer perceives in, or reads into, Bruegel's depiction. It is the force that moves his speaker to enter not only into the dynamics of the chain reaction that pulls these men, one after the other, to their inevitable fall, but also into their concurrent thought processes. "Something is wrong," the third man in the chain is wondering, "what is it? – how easy it is for people who can see ..." (line 17):

> Der Sog beginnt. Der zweite hat den Halt am Stock verloren,
> ...
> Der [dritte] weiß noch nicht, er strengt sich an zu wissen:
> Da ist was – was? – wie leicht es Sehende haben ... (St. III, lines 14–17)

Their anguished mental reaction is rendered both directly, as in the example quoted above, and in the third person, as when the empathizing observer remarks that the fourth man would give anything to "see his hollow eyes out – if only he could!" (lines 19–20):

> Der ihm die Hand auf nur gefühlte Schulter legt, verhält,
> Zögert und denkt: da ist Bewegung, die zieht mich – oh, er möchte sich
> Die leeren Augen aus dem Kopfe sehen – könnte er!
> Dann wäre alles gut. So ist's noch für die letzten fünf- und sechsten ...
> (St. III, lines 18–21)

The pictorial account, which can capture just one critical moment of the many that make up the process it sets out to portray, is brought to life imaginatively by the speaker's running commentary. Thanks to the different expressive potential of the poetic word, this commentary renders the action in both its outer and its inner dimension. Imperceptibly, the imagined interior monologue shifts back into objective observation, "so ist's noch für die letzten fünf- und sechsten" (line 21), displaying once again Bauer's mastery of perspectival nuance. The dramatic account rendered in the third section of the poem ends, in characteristic fashion, with a couplet mustering the combined forces of structured rhetoric and graphic metaphor. "Vom ersten bis zum letzten fließt die Woge aus, / Vom letzten bis zum ersten wächst sie in der Finsternis" (st. III, lines 24–5).

The fourth and concluding section of the poem picks up the introductory theme that describes the background against which the scene of the tumbling blind men is set in Bruegel's picture – a beautiful, serene day in beautiful Flanders:

> Und dann, an einem schönen Tag im schönen Flandern,
> Der Himmel ganz leicht blau von sanftem Licht, die Erde ruht,
> So still der Aufschlag einer Frucht, die fällt, würde gehört ...
> (St. III, lines 1–3)

The repetition is almost word for word:

> Alles in großer Stille und an einem schönen Tag, die Erde ruht,
> Und wer im Licht geht und im Licht sieht, hat es gut
> ...
> So still. Der Aufschlag einer Frucht, die fällt, würde gehört ...
>
> (St. IV, lines 1–2; 4)

Just as the blind men's passage into growing darkness is placed in Bruegel's visual presentation in the bright setting of "a beautiful day," so Bauer's poetic recreation is framed by a similarly contrasting verbal description. Following immediately are reflections on the scene thus brought to the reader's (or the viewer's) attention. They begin with a startling contrast: "So still. Der Aufschlag einer Frucht, die fällt, würde gehört, / Doch hat der Fall der Bettler nichts am Tag verstört" (st. IV, lines 4–5). The stillness that would make audible the sound of falling fruit will absorb the sound of falling men! The earth neither hears nor sees them; and if she does, it is without emotion because the blind led by the blind are bound to fall: "Wie Blinde fallen müssen, die ein Blinder führt" (line 7). The moralistic overtone of this conclusion is softened by the caveat, added immediately – Bauer's cautious reassurance: "Geduld: sie werden von dem Sturz, den sie getan, schon wieder aufstehn, / Sich sammeln, Staub abstreifen und im Dunkeln weitergehn" (st. IV, lines 8–9). Inevitably, we are told, man will stumble and fall and pick himself up again, and continue doing so in the darkness he cannot escape.

The medium of this universal message is the empathy sensed by Bauer in Bruegel's "record" and inscribed emphatically in his own. Such empathy moves the poet to view the sixteenth-century pictorial rendering of the biblical image, not as a negative example, but as a depiction of shared circumstance and experience, whose principal intention is to foster an awareness of the fellowship in the dark enjoyed and endured by all.

The sameness that levels all humanity is the subject of the highly rhetorical piece "Die Stimme" (LL 125). "Your voice" (line 19) and "my voice" (line 20) are "the same voice" (line 21), whether they are heard as the "innocent" voice of the child (lines 1–3), the "pure" voice of the young lover (lines 4–6), the "distorted" voice of the adult murderer (lines 8–10), or the "desolate" voice of the dying (lines 12–14) about to fall silent and be buried (lines 16–17). "Ecce Homo!" is what these twenty-one lines exclaim in Bauer's superbly unassuming words: this is how we go through life – in turn vulnerable, loving, murderous, ultimately alone, and soon forgotten. The challenge extended to the reader is again to recognize shared potential, shared guilt, shared waste, and to draw the appropriate consequences:

Es war die gleiche Stimme.
Es war deine Stimme.
Es war meine Stimme.
Es war die gleiche Stimme. (Lines 18–21)

> *"Dennoch erklären wir beide*
> *diese Tage zu den ersten der Welt."*

I now come to what I would suggest is Bauer's humanistic *carpe diem* that forms part of his latterday *vanitas mundi* idea. Given the blind and misguided, ultimately futile ways of the world, but given also the seeds of goodness that reside in every human being, our chance lies in making the best of our gift of humanity during the short time we have at our disposal.

The basis for the attitude Bauer strives to promote is a sensitive awareness and appreciation of the surrounding world, both natural and human. The most effective teacher in this regard, short of need, is the absence of things we tend to take for granted. The poem "Belehrung aus arktischen Gebieten" (*LL* 93) shows that the icy surroundings and the strain they impose even on an involuntary physical function such as breathing, generate an awareness of what the earth really is:

Daß man dort im Eis
Und bei unaufhörlicher Anstrengung noch des Atmens
Sich dessen bewußt werde, was Erde sei. (Lines 4–6)

Extreme conditions, "where there is nothing" and "where nothing comes easy" (lines 10–11), sharpen one's senses to the "magic," (line 12) which the earth holds in store; they enable us to perceive the "miracle" (line 18) that has produced the beauty of something as familiar as a flower (lines 17–18).

A mind thus sensitized takes pleasure in the "tiefes Entzücken blattloser Zeit" (line 4), as the beautiful little piece, "Heute morgen" (*LL* 104; *KN* 31), demonstrates. Such nature poetry is rare in Bauer's work. Significantly, it, too, reveals this poet's all-embracing human perspective. The "pearls of ice" on the wintry tree are fruit ("die schönsten Früchte," line 1) ready for human consumption. Anthropomorphic images are employed to conclude the poem. The light of noon, with "a warm hand," "carefully separated" the fruit from the branches, and they fell into "the lap of the earth":

Gegen Mittag
Streifte die warme Hand des Lichtes
Wie die Hand eines Obstpflückers
Die Früchte vorsichtig ab.
Blitzend fielen sie der Erde in den Schoß. (Lines 9–13)

A mind thus sensitized draws connections between the natural and the human world. Observing the autumnal flight of birds, the speaker in the poem "Sieh auf – am kühlen großen Himmel" (LL 102; KN 71), by way of contrast, "hears the steps of the prisoner"; he is reminded immediately and acutely of the restricted movements of a person kept in a confined, possibly solitary place:

Da ich die Späherblicke
Zum Raum der großen Vogelflüge hebe,
Hör ich die Schritte des Gefangenen klingen,
Fühl ich, wie mir die Pfeile tief ins Herzfleisch dringen. (St. IV)

He may well have in mind the condition of the human being on earth.

A mind thus sensitized receives creative inspiration from the sight "of the first cherry tree / in the rosy snow" – a precious find "carried" from the window onto the piece of paper on the poet's desk ("Beginn des großen Gesanges," LL 89–90, st. I). The narrative introduction provided by the first stanza is followed by seemingly pure nature poetry that brings to life the wintry scene and what its finely observed and imagined processes serve to herald. This particular tree has shaken off more snow than the others, thus leading them by one stanza in the great chorus they are about to begin (st. II); the other trees in turn hurry (st. III) to launch the "music of green" (st. IV) which finally touches off "the great chorus" (st. V):

Noch mehr Schnee,
Leuchtender noch,
War aus dem Schwarz der Äste
Hervorgebrochen.
Horch: er ist allen anderen Bäumen
Um eine Strophe im großen Gesang
Voraus. (St. II, lines 3–9)

Doch nun
Beeilen sie sich... (St. III, lines 1–2)

Und nun
die Musik des Grün ... (St. IV, lines 1–2)

Und nun
Der große Gesang. (St. V)

This poem, however, is an allegory which in Bauer's dramatizing fashion records the process of intense observation and minute perception that precedes the birth of a poem. Relevant in the present context is not so much this poem's romantic tenor – grounded in formulations such as "Ein Hauch von rosigem Glühen noch / Im durchsichtigen Blau" (st. III, lines 8–9); or in expressive devices such as the synesthesia of the image "Musik des Grün" (st. IV, line 2). Relevant here is the concluding turn from the realm of nature to that of man, with the blackbird, like the man on the ship's mast, calling out "land!":

Noch die Amsel
Singt es aus wie der Späher
Im Maste des Schiffes:
Ich habe Land gesehen: Grün! (St. IV, lines 3–6)

The biblical associations that may come to the reader's mind indicate the redemptive power of "the great paean" launched by the imaginative process the poem has described. The conclusion to be drawn is this: by using his gifts of observation and expression, the person endowed with them – the poet, the artist – will responsibly "seize the day."

High as a keen awareness and sensitive use of the offerings of nature may range on Bauer's scale of values, the most important things by far are due awareness and appreciation of any gifts received within the human realm, followed by appropriate action. Not even the smallest and most ordinary pleasure in daily life is to be overlooked. This is the object lesson rendered by the poem, "Was ein freier Tag mir gibt" (LL 109). The natural flow and simplicity of the six short stanzas convey effectively the speaker's sense of ease and of being at one with himself and the world:

Gern und nachlässig bewege ich mich
Durch die Welt

Und verstreue, großherzig mit mir selber,
Meine Zeit. (St. VI)

This sense flows from his mindful enjoyment of the physical and
mental well-being experienced on a "free day." His body and mind,
like sentient beings, are grateful for the generous allowance of
rest (st. I-II); inside and outside are felt to be "aufgeräumt," both
"tidy" and "cheerful" (st. III, lines 1–2). No protective barriers are
needed, since the "shadows" that may intrude on such a day are
insubstantial:

Die vier Wände meines Zimmers
Sind durchlässig geworden,
Alles kommt herein, ohne zu verletzen,
Durchsichtig schweben heute die Schatten. (St. IV)

These lines subtly suggest a juxtaposition of this private moment
of gratefully embraced pleasure with the normal reign of dark forces
in the world at large. The poem "Dennoch" (*LL* 88) makes the point
that atrocities are being perpetrated everywhere, but the love
between two individuals is almost like an act of defiance that resets
the clock of the world: "Dennoch erklären wir beide / diese Tage zu
den ersten der Welt," (st. I, lines 4–5). The second stanza goes on to
elaborate in disturbing detail man's raging inhumanity (lines 1–4)
which – and this is the point – cannot stop "us two" from starting
our day "in schönem Einverständnis" (lines 5–6). But in spite of the
contrast thus hammered home, the walls that protect this private
peace are not impervious:

Es ist nicht sicher, wie lange wir leben werden
...
Armeen stehen an den Grenzen, ungeheure Wolken
sprechen von verborgenen Mitteln – (St. III, lines 1; 4–5)

The reference to an imminent invasion by the universal forces of
destruction ("armies at the borders," line 5), while pointing up a real
possibility, brings out more emphatically the poem's concluding
affirmation of interpersonal harmony:

Dennoch haben wir Freude aneinander, als blieben wir ewig beisammen,
und leben in einem guten Geheimnis.
Dennoch lieben wir uns. (St. III, lines 7–9)

Living in, and acting upon, such a "good secret" is the appropriate, if modestly effective, measure to counter the negativity of the forces abroad. Needless to add that the love relationship here given as a model may be replaced by any personal association informed by friendship and goodwill.

Awareness, appreciation, and reciprocation of gifts received from fellow human beings close or distant, alive or dead, are praised in the poem "Kein Unterschied mehr" (LL 124). Clearly spoken with Bauer's own voice, it invokes, with a single introductory stroke, the authority of life experience and reflection: "Schließlich / War kein Unterschied mehr" (lines 1–2). This is to pave the way for the speaker's subsequent denial of received hierarchical thinking. While accredited philosophers or artists (such as Plato and Tu Fu, lines 3–5) are generally, regarded more highly than ordinary students (lines 8–9), and political activists (such as the conspirators of July 20, lines 6–7) are deemed to be more important than simple cleaning women (lines 10–14), he declares their equal value in terms of what ultimately matters: human cooperation and mutual helpfulness:

Es war kein Unterschied mehr
Zwischen ihnen, Höhe und Tiefe
Glichen sich aus und gaben das gleiche,
Sie alle machten es mir möglich, zu leben,
Sie gehörten zusammen, sie gaben
Meinem Leben die Richtung, die Kraft.
So auch ich gehörte ihnen,
Ihnen allen. (Lines 15–22)

The concluding phrase – "In the same way I, too, belong to all of them" – is significant in that it points up the reciprocity of the human enterprise and the personal awareness and responsibility this entails.

As the poem "Zu einem Neger" (LL 101; KN 15) tells us in no uncertain terms, social reality presents a different picture. In all parts of the world, human beings have failed and continue to fail human beings, whether on the grounds of colour (st. I), religion (st. II) or ethnicity (st. III). Cast into the mould of a first-person account, the four stanzas of this poem, aided by parallel construction, point an unforgiving finger at all those guilty of silence and inaction. Relentlessly, the speaker castigates himself for his own failure to convey to the victims of prejudice and insensitivity his sense of collective guilt and personal shame. One stanza will suffice to demonstrate this:

Zu einem Neger,
Der mir entgegenkam:
Verzeih mir deine Verfolgung überall,
Verzeih mir, daß du keine Wohnung findest in weißen Bezirken. –
Ich sagte es nicht.
Er ging vorüber. (St. I)

Varying the pattern of the three "exemplifying" stanzas, the concluding stanza fires a powerful charge of self-accusation, intended as a model for those who are less self-critical:

Zu einem,
Der mir entgegenkam:
Dir verzeihe ich nichts.
Zu einem Stummen, den ich erkannte:
Dir wird nichts vergeben. –
Ich sagte es zu mir. (St. IV)

To read this poem merely as an expression of Bauer's own sense of guilt would be to miss much of its scope and intention. Grounded as it is in autobiographial fact, the "I"-account serves to lend substance to the example here given of opportunity unused, time not seized, life wasted.

This is the topic explicitly and expansively laid out in the poem "Eines Tages werden wir aufwachen und wissen" (LL 92; NT 75). Poetically of little interest, this piece spells out Bauer's concern and regret. All that will remain, he concludes, is a vague memory that once there was something which held promise; we, however, have wasted our time pitifully – to reap nothing but ashes:

Wir werden uns erinnern, daß da etwas war voller Verheißung,
...
Nur: daß da etwas war, dem wir nicht folgten –
Und hinzufügen: daß wir keine Zeit hatten, leider –
Weil wir die Zeit vergeudeten in kleiner, abgegriffener Münze.
Und von dem Aufblitzen des Lichtes und dem Windhauch blieb nichts.
Nur Asche. (St. II, lines 8; 11–15)

Using the first person plural, Bauer clearly signals the universality of his perspective and the inclusiveness of his implied call to remedial action.

The preceding discussions have shown that Bauer's treatment of the *carpe diem* theme steers clear of the hedonistic element that one usually associates with this notion. While the idea of pleasure is not at all absent from his thinking, it is based entirely on the foundation of his humanistic assumptions. In his scheme of things, pleasure derives not so much from a self-centred enjoyment of what the moment may have to offer, as it does from actively embracing interpersonal commitment and responsibility. At a time when existentialist anguish occupied the minds of his fellow Germans, and material progress those of his fellow Canadians, the deep concern of Bauer's poetry inevitably fell on deaf ears.

The Courage of Old Age

⫷ *"At seventy I began to remould my life."*

When Bauer, on his publisher's suggestion, decided to mark his seventieth birthday with the issue of his retrospective *Lebenslauf*, he approached the task of compiling it with mixed feelings. On the one hand, he was proud of being the only one among his (by now very few) contemporaries who could present such a volume; he was confident that every one of these poems would be a worthwhile document arresting in crafted form one specific moment of life: "Had it been worthwhile? Certainly. Every poem ... holds one formed moment of life, my life at a certain point in time. I thought that none of my contemporaries – there weren't very many left – could come up with such a volume" (23 June 1974).[1]

On the other hand, he harboured no illusions about the reception awaiting his poetry. "I don't believe the volume would 'go,' most likely crawl," he wrote to his friend and fellow poet Henry Beissel (12 November 1973).[2] And when the volume had appeared, the cloud of scepticism grew darker still. This is what Bauer put down in his diary: "It [my volume] won't be noticed. And why should it? Why should it be noticed – and by whom? It's dried-up leaves" (8 June 1975).[3] The concluding simile is significant. As dried-up leaves once were fresh foliage, so the poems, now judged to be old and lifeless, were alive and meaningful at the time that they document.

Such historical thinking, however, fosters the tenacious stance taken by the septuagenarian in the face of indifference and rejection. *Lebenslauf*, he said to himself, was "interesting – and passé" ("interessant – und vorbei," 9 August 1974); it was his farewell (5 June 1975) that brought something to a close – "einen 'deutschen' Lebenslauf" (23 May 1975). It was the *German* part of his life as a poet which Bauer hoped to put *ad acta* with this publication. His pen, however, was not to rest: "But you still have chances – : one chance. The radical turn of your old age. No matter what the results will be. This turn is still possible" (8 June 1975).[4]

His diaries bear witness to his complex attitude of self-criticism, self-assurance, and dogged determination: "I am fed up with myself. All of it sentimental and forced; all of it without momentum, without strength. Do you know who you are: an old man. Wake up, drowsy-head – I have woken up" (15 June 1974).[5] In September of the same year he reaffirmed the positive turn pronounced at the end of the entry just quoted: "There are *old masters*: underline both" ("Es gibt alte Meister: beides unterstreichen," 6 September 1974). Bauer was here picking up a thread he had begun to spin earlier that year: "I know what kind of poems I should and could write; but I still hesitate. Don't hesitate too long … Masculine poetry" (12 March 1974). And: "The great poems are still to come. ----------------- When no one thought he would do anything worthwhile – he came into his own" (18 April 1974).[6]

The use of the English language in this private document is revealing: obviously Bauer had in mind an English-speaking readership that he planned to surprise. He was in fact working on a novel in English, using as its title the familiar and telling phrase "S'en aller!" His new "great" and "masculine" poetry was probably to be composed in his adopted language, too. On 27 September 1976, two months before his death, he wrote in his diary: "He who has stepped out of the daily life of his language must step into that of his new language."[7] In light of all this, his unexpected death seems to take on a tragic dimension: his new novellistic work was nipped in the bud, and the "great poems – unwritten" ("große Gedichte – ungeschrieben," 19 April 1974), by the evidence of what has been published, were to remain largely unwritten.

After the publication of *Lebenslauf* in the spring of 1975, Bauer cannot have produced very many poems. As Beissel explains in his essay on Bauer's unpublished manuscripts, the majority of the approximately six hundred unpublished poems date back to the decade before 1973. In the diary of his last year, excerpts from which have been translated by Henry Beissel, there are a number of entries that speak of a growing sense of fatigue, physical and mental:

Feb. 23
Winter; cold. Exhausted in spite of the reading week during which I went to my office every morning to catch up and to prepare. How happy shall I be when it's all over (TR 43),

writes the dedicated teacher. And further:

June 19
Indolence, numbness: *dullness*. Worked on and off but without engagement. That too is old age. (TR 47)

July 2
Tiredness easily leads to revulsion. It's waiting at the corner. Be watchful. (TR 48)

July 5
In spite of your revulsion you must eat if you want to live. Basically, everything is reduced to a simple question: do you want to carry on or don't you? Since the answer is affirmative, you must do your best. (TR 49)

July 9
The Olympic Games move towards their disaster. – This dull exhaustion of my brain. (TR 49)

July 11
Your feeling unwell has *one* reason: indecisiveness. Low spirits make indolent. (TR 49)

August 16
First thinking gets tired. Then the flesh follows. Be watchful. (TR 52)

Nov. 16
Tuesday; a beautiful bright November day. Slowly I seem to have come out from under a state of tiredness which completely demoralized me. Cassandra suffers from chronic hoarseness. She has fallen silent. (TR 57)

Nov. 19
Friday. How radiant these November mornings. Every one of them delays the coming of winter. But I myself am not radiant.
A few short letters. Persistent nausea. (TR 58)

Nov. 26
Yesterday a bad day. I felt paralyzed. Read Scott Fitzgerald's *The Last Tycoon* in bed. So so. (TR 59)

Nov. 28
Sunday. Grey, cold. Not good; too exhausted to do anything. Where does this exhaustion come from? (TR 59)

These constant expressions of tiredness and exhaustion seem to imply more than "the nostalgia and weariness of an aging man" (Beissel, UPM 193). They may well have been the signs of Bauer's approaching death which, when it arrived on December 23, seemed so sudden. The barrage of self-exhortation and self-encouragement, which this fiercely determined aging man kept up to the very end – "At seventy-two I began to remould my life" was the updated birthday version of his life-sustaining motto (4 November 1976; TR 56) – this tireless goading and reassuring seems to have been just the reverse side of the same coin.

⨳ *"Die großen Gedichte kommen noch."*

Bauer's last diary entry points in the direction of a possible inspirational model for the "great masculine" poetry he still wanted to write: "A. is right: I mention Brecht too often" (28 November 1976; TR 59). The exemplar here acknowledged, if indirectly by means of (ironic?) negation, was not the activist Brecht, whose political poems Bauer found "naive" (29 August 1976), but Brecht, the master of precision: "Work out a concept of poetry that combines the sharpness of Brecht, the urbanity of W.H. Auden, the vast yet never dissolving gesture of St. John Perse. Wouldn't this mean mixing fire and water? Not at all."[8] A similar remark entered into his diary just a few months prior to that fateful December 23 serves to reaffirm the admiration of Brecht's poetic craft which Bauer took into his grave: "sharpness of the knife; precision of a Chinese brush drawing – precision need not lead to a shortness that stifles the breath and is deadly."[9]

Immediately following, we find this masterpiece of sharpness, precision, and brevity that surely does not stifle the breath and kill:

Einst, jetzt:
Als ich sie traf,
War sie schön.
Nach 25 Jahren
Ist sie viel schöner:
Damals sagten es viele.
Jetzt bin ich es, der es sagt. (29 August 1976)

A quarter century of growing appreciation and closeness between two people is encapsulated in these minimal lines. Their finely chiselled texture of contrasts serves to marry bare concision with rich suggestiveness. The title, in maximum brevity, juxtaposes the situation as it was then with the situation as it is now, exploiting the connotative power of the poetic "einst" to remove the "then" to an indistinct and remote realm of past unreality. This frame of reference serves to prepare a proper understanding of the implications conveyed by the startling contrast between the beauty of her youth and the even greater beauty of her later years: the former was and is less real, less true than the latter. A parallel contrast follows to point up, by way of explanation, the difference between "outer" and "inner" beauty, the former easily recognized by all and readily used as a means of labelling and judging, the latter perceived and appreciated only by the person who over the years has earned access to the inner chambers of his partner's real self. In turn, her "beauty" has grown in the soil of mutual commitment and caring, cultivated over the years within the carefully guarded enclosure of intimacy.

A love poem of precision and power, does this piece give us a taste of the poetry Bauer aimed to write but ran out of time to produce in greater number? The poem with which Henry Beissel decided to close his account of Bauer's unpublished poetry provides another thought-provoking glimpse. Dated 26 June 1976, it is probably one of his last poems. Here it is in full:

Leichtere Zeit

Hell, das ich staunend sah,
Ist überwundene Nacht;
Deshalb, hab ich bedacht,
Freut mich das Sommerjahr.

Nichts ist gelöst, ich weiß,
Doch wie ich gehe jetzt,
Scheine ich unverletzt,
Atmend belebenden Preis:

Atem *ist* Lobgesang
Dieser zu kurzen Frist.
Heut trägt er mich leicht entlang.
Ich bin, weil er ist. (UPM 194)

Its precision is such that everything, down to the individual letter or accent, matters.

The poem possesses a clear and simple rhyme scheme that falls short of perfection by just one slight impurity ("sah" – "-jahr" [st. 1, lines 1 and 4]). "Rhyme," as Beissel explains, "is something Bauer took up seriously ... during the summer of 1968"; it is found in all but five of the seventy-three poems gathered in his last poetry manuscript "Atemzüge" of 1971 (UPM 185). Bauer may well have embraced it as an agent of order to counter the ravages of unreason ("Stupidität") that came to weigh more and more on his mind. Employed to this end, rhyme is more than ornament; it serves the important function of highlighting aspects of the form and content of the poem.

First, rhyme differentiation throws into relief a division of the poem into two unequal parts. Stanzas I and II, grouped together by enclosing rhyme, consider the profound ambivalence of the human condition: one needs negative experience to see the good things and appreciate them (st. I); one has no answers or solutions but may attain, through wise acquiescence, a sense or an illusion of well-being (st. II). Stanza III, set apart by alternating rhyme, concludes that "being," i.e., survival under these conditions, is predicated on a positive acceptance and active celebration of this twofaced, yet all too short term of life.

Secondly, all rhymes but one are masculine. They endow the poem with a structural firmness that keeps in check the deep emotions it calls up. The stressed line endings, in conjunction with the stressed line beginnings, provide emphatic points of rest which slow down the pace of reading and prompt the reader to consider carefully every particle incorporated into this lean poetic structure. Thus, for example, one pauses to ponder the implications of the pregnant prefix "be-" (st. I, line 3); or the meaning of the puzzling compound "Sommerjahr" (st. I, line 4); or the reason, beyond rhyme, for the placement of the adverb "jetzt" after the dependent verb "gehe" (st. II, line 2); or the implications of the dual reference performed by the pronoun "er" (st. III, line 4).

Such reflective "Zeilenstil" clearly dominates the first two stanzas. It tightens their smooth rhythmic alternation and prevents an all too easy flow that might have compromised the seriousness of the thoughts here expressed. In the concluding stanza, the taut frame is opened up through enjambement (from line 1, which possesses the poem's only unstressed rhyme syllable, to line 2); and through the extended verse (line 3). The flow here released, particularly in line 3, serves as an apt medium for what these lines express: for today, my celebration in word of the time I have will carry me along with ease. As if to hammer home that such "leichtere Zeit" can be enjoyed only briefly, a sharply contrasting, highly condensed final line serves, in conclusion, to restore firmly the poem's characteristic intellectual discipline.

Finally, the poem comes with a significant title. This latter is not simply a line, usually the first, borrowed for editorial ease or indifferent description. Rather, it offers the essence of the conclusion to be drawn from the thoughts developed, line after line, by the three stanzas in their particular configuration. The conclusion to be drawn is this: our short "time" will become "easier" if we recognize it for what it is, accept and affirm it. The message is simple enough, but it was extracted in a long process of hard reflection. While the body of the poem, tightly packed with denotation and richly endowed with connotation, engages the reader in an intense effort to pinpoint exactly what seems so clear, the title serves both as a beacon guiding the way and as a fire signal drawing attention to itself.

Bauer's thoughtful and emphatic use of titles in a good number of his later poems was first noted, of course, by Henry Beissel, who in the relevant context tells us that "the poems are also more carefully crafted" (UPM 175). The present example offers insight into what is new in Bauer's formative effort. My explorations of his poetry have shown that he has always paid meticulous attention to the fashioning of poetic form. In this he used to rely largely on rhetorical devices as means of order and emphasis. Whether he had in hand a long poem or a short one, it was basically a matter of arranging for specific effect words and phrases that were duplicated, multiplied and varied in a number of ways – sometimes with considerable results. In composing the two poems just considered, Bauer seems to have looked more critically at the components themselves, paring them down to their core and making them deliver their unadorned essential message in highly condensed, plain, but artfully assembled words and phrases, devoid of rhetoric, description, or overt didacticism. As a result, the poems are at once precise and suggestive, readily understood and yet impossible to paraphrase.

As Bauer's diary entry concerning his self-confessed over-preoccupation with Brecht would seem to suggest, an inspirational stimulus for the sparse expressiveness marking these two poems may well have emanated from some of Brecht's poetry. And yet another "model" may have gained entry into Bauer's poetic workshop: "There is *one* form of courage: that of old age. – Yesterday afternoon read the marvellous poems of Gottfried Benn – poems, melancholy, verses – and was deeply moved. Apart from the early Brecht (and a few of his later poems), nothing can match them; not in tone, not in fulness of existence" (23 February 1976; transl. Henry Beissel, TR 44). While Bauer in earlier years had no patience with the nihilism and self-indulgent melancholy of Benn's "Artistik," life experience and accumulated disappointment may have brought him closer to the

thought and art of this supreme master of poetic form. Some perti-
nent observations found in Beissel's informative essay on Bauer's
unpublished poetry seem to point in this direction: "In his final col-
lection of poetry there is growing evidence that Bauer had profound
doubts about human existence," Beissel writes (UPM 186); "Bauer
agonized over the practical use of the arts, as other artists have"
(188); "Art provides an ironic form of transcendence" (188). It is hard
not to draw a connection to Benn's concept of the "transcendence of
creative pleasure" providing life-enabling, if temporary, relief from
the absurdities of the world (see Manyoni 232ff.). The poem "Leich-
tere Zeit" seems to confirm such an affinity. Its emphatic equation of
"Atem" and "Lobgesang" – of breathing (a necessary function of life)
and praising in song (affirming life through the creative act) – stands
in significant contrast to the preceding reflections on the profound
ambivalence of human existence. In prefacing his praise of Benn's
poems with a bow to "the courage of old age," was Bauer, then,
contemplating "the radical turn of [his own] old age" (8 June 1975)
that would make him draw the consequence of his darker insights,
and say things he had so far forbidden himself to say, and do so in
a manner he used to frown upon? Would any poetry written with
the courage of old age have realized his vision of "great masculine"
art? Would it have been "great" by objective standards? The two
poems discussed in the previous pages seem to point in the direction
of an affirmative answer.

> "Noble bird!
> You should have sung your dirge
> And died."

Walter Bauer, a man of his word, did begin to write in English. His
unfinished novel "S'en aller!" has already been mentioned. Writing
prose in a language acquired in adulthood is one thing; writing
poetry, surely, is another. The fact that Bauer resisted this challenge
for many years is evidence of his good sense as a poet. When he
finally did set out on this new venture, the results were quite
remarkable. Henry Beissel tells us that among the numerous uncol-
lected poems of Bauer's later years there are a "handful" of poems
written in English (UPM 194), some of which were published in the
posthumous *Tamarack Review.* I now turn to these eight pieces.

Selected by Henry Beissel, they enable us to sample in English the
variety of themes and forms that are the hallmark of Bauer's poetry.
Epigrammatic concision is found beside narrative expansiveness,
minimal lines beside long lines, single-stanza composition beside

cyclical configuration, statement beside suggestion – to name just some of the more obvious formal features. Thematically, too, these poems cover a wide but familiar territory: immigration, personal reflection, social criticism, thoughts on transient and immutable values, on art and language. Discussion will proceed in the thematic order just indicated.

"The Conqueror" (*TR* 31–4) is a well ordered sequence of ten numbered, highly stylized units of varying length. Description, question-and-answer, and summarizing comment are employed to present a portrait of the typical immigrant. The conqueror metaphor, unbroken throughout the entire sequence, provides the thematic material to highlight, both by contrast and identification, the salient features of the immigrant's life, aspiration, and success. Unit I, the longest in the sequence, serves as a narrative introduction stating the "significant" yet unnoticed arrival of the conqueror in the loyal company of his two hands. Structurally, these twenty-two lines are framed by introductory statement and concluding amplification of the important fact of arrival, the relevant lines being symmetrically reversed in the conclusion:

> The conqueror entered the city
> But no one noticed his arrival ... (i: lines 1–2)

> The land did not notice
> The significant arrival of the conqueror.
> But he has entered the city. (i: lines 20–2)

Units ii–viii employ parallel sequence of question-and–answer to assemble the various facets of this "conqueror's" undertaking: "And how ...?" (ii, iii, v); "And where ...?" (twice in iv); "And what ...?" (vi, viii); "And does ...?" (vii). Thus one learns that his "reign" consists of hard labour ten hours a day for the pleasure and comfort of others (ii). His "entourage" is made up of the old habits brought along from his country of origin, materially present in the form of bread, tomatoes, and onions for lunch (iii). His residence is a noisy rooming house, his private chamber a minimally furnished room for six dollars a week (iv). His evenings are spent studying the dictionary – the "bible" he needs for his conquest (v). His "pastimes" are the pleasures of regularly depositing his pay cheques (vi). The "decrees" he issues are the letters to his wife asking her to be patient until their joint conquest has been properly prepared (vii). The "messages" he sends out are monthly transfers of twenty dollars to his proud mother back home (viii). All this is presented in ironic fusion of allusion to historical conquest with allusion to contemporary "vip"-interviews on radio or television. Here is a short excerpt:

And what
Are the messages of the conqueror
From his city?
The monthly transfers
Of twenty dollars to his mother. (VIII: lines 1–5)

Units IX and X form the summary conclusion by the narrator or
interviewer who employs anaphora to bring out the "conqueror's"
most important qualities – patience, humility, and endurance:

He is patient like granite.
He humbles himself.
He bows down.
He is indestructible. (IX: lines 2–5)

Concluding the poem, sequential phrase repetition underscores the
universality of this "Nobody's" quest, implying also varying kinds
and degrees of success:

His name is Sisyphus.
His name is Ulysses.
His name is Colombus.
His name is Nobody. (X: lines 1–4)

Sisyphus was condemned to unending toil; Ulysses did arrive – after
many a shipwreck and many lives lost; Columbus found something
other than what he had set out to discover. The "conqueror's" even-
tual "success" is no doubt taking shape, thanks to his tireless efforts:
"His name is 'No English. Please.' / *Yet for the present only*"(lines 5–6;
emphasis added). But the preceding literary and historical allusions
caution against a false expectation of easy or immediate success.

The ambiguity thus introduced differentiates clearly Bauer's
English treatment of the immigration issue from the earlier versions
he wrote in German. The earlier negative stance has been softened
here to a stance which, while steering clear of blatant optimism, does
not issue a cry of "failure!" either. Whether it was due to lengthy
exposure to Canadian compromise and consideration, or to the mel-
lowing influence of advanced age, the ironic ambiguity injected into
the familiar Baueresque structure of this poem makes it an eminently
absorbing piece of poetic discourse.

Equally absorbing, although for different reasons, is the poem
"Mood at Dusk" (*TR* 30). It renders, in Bauer's carefully worded
rhythmic free verse, an intensely real flashback to the lost "secure
universe" of his childhood. Winter, dusk and old age (lines 1–2) all

signal the imminent end of a given period of time that invites retro-
spective reflection on its warmer, brighter and unharmed begin-
nings. "Feel[ing] his childhood lean against his heart" (line 7), the
old man finds himself surrounded by its sights, sounds, smells, pets
and toys; he sees the worn but loving hand of his mother; he relives
the boy's anticipation of his father's return from work (lines 8–19);
"Yes, his nostalgic heart sees, hears all of this / And for a moment's
miracle he feels secure" (lines 20–1). The spell is eventually broken
by the electric switch: as it lights the man's present world, it extin-
guishes that of his childhood:

> And so, at last, he reaches for the electric switch
> Which in a flash causes that world,
> That child-secure universe, to disappear. (Lines 23–5)

The nostalgia of this mental flashback is thrown into relief by
inverted contrast. Yesteryear's gay and harmless war toys are
brought into focus by the welcome absence of their modern techno-
logically inspired counterparts ("Toys free of space-ships, Men-from-
Mars – even of aeroplanes," line 15). Conversely, the oil lamps of
yore ("But then he sees too the oil-lamps waiting to be lit," line 22)
are annihilated by the click of a electric switch (line 23). While this
set of oppositions is well elaborated, the crucial contrast they serve
to accentuate is to be drawn by inference. There are two signals. The
statement, "this soft, strange world begins to free him of his present"
(line 6) suggests bondage to a time with which the man does not
identify. As one learns later, it is a time in which "feel[ing] secure"
is experienced as a "miracle" (line 21). At the end of the poem, the
composite adjective "child-secure" (line 25) reiterates the point: the
child felt secure, the old man does not. The vision which brings back
the secure universe of childhood that seems to return like a "long
lost friend" (line 3) only intensifies the old man's deeply saddened
sense of loss.

Rendering the disenchantment and nostalgia of old-age, this poem
appears to be an elegy written in the manner of modern restraint.
This genre allows the poet to express personal experience and senti-
ment without the risk of appearing to be caught in narrow subjectiv-
ity. It enables this poet, a committed citizen of the twentieth century,
to give voice to his deeply felt regret, without giving in to outmoded
poetic sentimentality. He does so through an unadorned description
of fact and detail that provides, in the place of guiding comment,
structural signals which point to what has not been said, but to what
is clearly the ultimate concern of the poem. The expressiveness thus

achieved is enhanced by the emotive intensity of the poem's rhythmic flow.

Similarly, the poem "In the Atomic Age" (TR 27) is made to speak through its form. It is a beautifully fashioned call "to detect in the rubble of material gains / the age-old loveliness of the world" (st. 1, lines 4–5) . It is a call to pause, to be alert, to resist the hardening of the heart "in this dangerous hour" (st. 1, lines 12–14); it is a call to listen "for the soundless footfall of truth / and beauty's eternal voice" (st. 11, lines 2–3). It is hard to resist the temptation of citing the entire piece, for it is through its exquisite choice of word, phrase, and image, together with a finely attuned rhythm, that the "eternal" values of truth and beauty are defended and affirmed. Thematically, this is familiar ground: the march of materialism and destructiveness must be halted, urges the poet, and to do this we must sensitize ourselves to the difference between false and real values, and sharpen our receptivity to the latter. Significantly, this admonition lacks any trace of reproach or accusation. The danger is coming not from within, but from without – from the "crude ways" of the "Atomic Age." They "terrify" the heart that must therefore be protected from self-defensive, in essence self-destructive "hardening" (line 13). Again, one notes a softening of stance: the compassionate critic has become a compassionate guardian and teacher.

Drawing attention to "beauty's eternal voice," this teacher directs the reader to art as the realm where the immutable touches this world of transience and death. In twelve mainly long lines, the poem "Painted Floor in Tell El Amarna" (TR 29) elaborates on the well-worn theme of "mortal things of any kind fall[ing] into ruin" (line 7), and of things created by art being "deathless" (line 8) and ever ready to take flight on the wings of the recreative imagination:

Yet, look: unhurt by arrows, deathless a wild duck
Rises from papyrus and rush
And soon with winds or stillness will begin its winged play. (Lines 8–10)

Baroque and romantic thinking are here reentering the scene hand in hand, reminding the reader of the mortality which not even a "god-prince" (such as the "great king Akenaton" [line 3]) can escape, and offering solace in the fact that a creature as humble as a wild duck may enter eternity through its depiction in art.

Not only does art arrest its subject-matter in lasting form that may be brought to life imaginatively, it lends expression and thus renders testimony to the human being's intuitive knowledge of a world greater than ours. The short poem "Botticelli's Women" (TR 25) speaks of "another world – / a perfect world, unknown / but felt with longing intuition" (lines 7–9). The "women" of the title are the painter's live models and their pictorial images fused into one. This double perspective provides the basis for the poem's climactic juxtaposition of the creatures of art with those of life, the former possessing the vision that is denied to the latter:

> For, blind, they yet behold
> A heavenly realm of beauty
> Forever hidden from them while they live. (Lines 13–15)

The vision can only have been given to them by the artist, who is thus proclaiming his own. The question of whether Bauer on his part entered Boticelli's creative mind with the objectivity of an art historian, or with the sentivity of a fellow artist, does not seem hard to answer. His tendency elsewhere to link his portraiture of artists and other great men to his own life, thought and work (see Riedel, "Künstler-Porträts" and "Biographien") suggests empathy and agreement. This would accord well with his advocacy of "old virtues" and attendant old values.

A good measure of empathy will have moved him to compose the thirteen evocative lines on a great fellow poet's tragic fate; the poem is titled "Hölderlin – the Swan-Ghost" (TR 26). The surprising compound "swan-ghost," instead of the familiar "swan-song," immediately catches the reader's attention. It signals a departure from the traditional association with the dying song of this "noble bird": the enticing thought of poetic/artistic perfection reached just before the moment of death, crowned by it, and followed by no decline. As the poem explains with the restraint of deeply felt regret, this crowning experience was denied to the poet addressed here. He was one of Germany's greatest poets, who at the age of thirty-seven descended into the darkness of mental illness, never to recover before his death thirty-six years later. "Dead" (line 13) as a poet, and like a "ghost" not admitted to its rest,

> You floated tragically on
> And on,
> … over the grave of your hopes and
> Your life … (lines 8–11).

As the poem suggests, the cause of this horrendous fate lay in a fatal essential link between the creative genius and dark superior forces: "But you and the sombre waters / Were wed" (lines 4–5). This idea has exercised many minds in the course of the history of German art and thought, particularly those gathered under the umbrella of romanticism. As I have argued above, Bauer, in picking up the thread, must have been moved to do so by a measure of shared insight, and a sense of affinity (cf. Riedel, "Künstler-Porträts" 81).

The tradition-laden swan metaphor serves as a richly evocative poetic medium. The "waters," the swan's element, are at once "sombre" (line 4) and "hallowed" (line 12), providing "life" (line 11) and "hopes" (line 10), but allowing him only to "skim" his "dream" and his "song" – and this "forever" (lines 6–7), never reaching the fulfilment of his last crowning song. This brings to mind an intriguing thought: is this a glimpse of a fear or premonition Bauer may have had about the fate of his own creativity?

As if to honour Hölderlin's classically oriented poetic craftsmanship, Bauer presents his tribute in kindred poetic form. Six rhythmically smooth longer lines possessing three stressed syllables alternate regularly with five short lines possessing two syllables and one stress. All short lines end in the stressed syllable that marks important points to ponder: "and *died* " (line 3), "were *wed* " (line 5), "your *song* " (line 7), "and *on* " (line 9), "your *life* " (line 11; my emphases). With two exceptions, the long lines end in an unstressed syllable that carries the rhythmic flow into the next verse (lines 4, 6, 10, 12). A stressed ending occurs twice, providing emphasis and deictic retardation: "You should have sung your dirge / And died" (lines 2–3) and "You floated tragically on / And on" (lines 8–9). All this is framed by the three stressed monosyllables: the emotionally laden address at the beginning: "Noble bird!" (line 1), and the sharply pointed end: "Dead" (line 13). The metric finesse of this poem is complemented by a finely woven texture of alliteration and assonance. Writing such poetry in an adopted language can only be described as a remarkable achievement.

The poet who seems intent on trimming his poetic language down to its core in order to expose and employ the beauty of its bare essentials aptly considers the wisdom that lay behind the use of hieroglyphs. The poem "Hieroglyphs" (*TR* 28) begins with a contrast that serves to accentuate the speaker's – i.e., the poet's – differently apportioned disgust and admiration: disgust at the contemporary "morass of words" which questionable sophistication turns into half-truths or lies of assorted colours (lines 1–2); admiration of what "the Egyptians of old so splendidly did" with their pictorial signs (lines 4–5). Of particular significance to him are "the precision and / unequivocal clarity of a hand moving slowly to say: / this is a duck flying, a sleeping child" (lines 6–8). These essential messages were carved out carefully, precisely and clearly, and "nothing more need be said" (line 11). The images thus produced are "immutable sign[s] for ... primal fact[s]" (line 15) that have the power to "touch" and to generate live connections in the onlooker's mind and heart:

How it touches me to see this old man standing for
all those who must count their springs.
Neighbour in life's late season: How are you? (Lines 12–14)

This seems to be the gist of the aging poet's *ars poetica*. Alerted already to Bauer's new-found appreciation of the art of Gottfried Benn, one notes a striking resemblance to some central tenets of Benn's poetological thinking. Bauer's pictorial sign of a "primal fact" touching off mental connections seems to be akin to Benn's "primal word" yielding "primal vision" and with it an array of associations (Manyoni 131). What separates the two positions is a profound intellectualism on the one side, and a profound humanism on the other. Benn, the *poeta doctus*, works with associations predicated on knowledge; Bauer, the *poeta humanus*, reaches out to his "neighbour" in word, thought, and sentiment.

Returning to the text in hand, the speaker spells out the point of his preceding deliberations: "One could learn from these Egyptians of old how to be / careful with words and to know what things and seasons are" (lines 16–17).

The poem concludes with a thought-provoking quotation from Virgil adduced, presumably, to signal a landmark in the change of attitude to language from ancient wisdom to contemporary abuse: "Lacrimae rerum sunt" (line 19). What language expresses and communicates, namely human experience, is inherently saturated with tears. The Egyptians "knew" but were wise enough to use a kind of "language" that would stick to basic facts and leave the saddening implications unspoken. Some considerable time later, Virgil came and "voiced" (line 20), that is to say put into words, his sad insight into the nature of human experience and the sorry task of language:

They knew a good deal, these people. They also knew:
Lacrimae rerum sunt.
But this is Virgil's voice, and it is much later. (Lines 18–20)

Even though Virgil's dictum is itself a splendid example of "careful" wording, it is a comment that goes well beyond "hieroglyphic" statement of plain fact. At this point, it seems, restraint was loosened and developments were unleashed that would eventually bring about the "morass" of calculated imprecision and abuse in which we are caught today. A responsible user of words is now obliged to under-take a daily cleanup: "every day I make it my duty to clean some of them for my own use" (line 3).

At first glance, the medium seems to contradict the message. The style and the tone of the poem are deliberately conversational. Here is another typical passage: "They had pictorial signs, these Egyp-tians, this was their written language. / Quite an achievement, if one considers ..." (lines 5–6). Why did Bauer, in considering and praising a careful use of necessary words, adopt a language utterly devoid of stylization, a language purposely chatty? On reflection, he appears to have undertaken just one other kind of essential reduction – a reduction of his medium to its communicative function. For this effect, a conversational setting is suggested and an avuncular tone injected here and there, both of which give rise to a sense of benev-olent wisdom being issued from the chair by the fireside. The cryptic quotation from Virgil only adds to the aura of wise tutoring, and this in turn helps to prime the reader's willingness to decode the mes-sage. Thus again, Bauer's distinctly humane voice is heard – and its message gladly considered.

A more obvious example of "hieroglyphic" precision and clarity is the intensely poetic miniature "Lines":

> The rain falls as it ever falls
> Among the night's dark leaves
> But the heart within
> Is somehow changed,
> And for that change
> It strangely grieves. (TR 26)

Against the backdrop of the comforting stability of cyclical nature, the persona gives voice to his own perplexed grief in the face of vaguely understood changes within. One recognizes the melancholy of old age, its sense of loss in view of the changes (a hardening?) the heart has undergone over the years of cumulative experience. Those who have looked into Bauer's last diaries will recognize specifically the saddened voice of Bauer himself who saw, and endeavoured to resist, the progressive erosion of his firm belief in the human heart.

The poem bears witness to this personally experienced "primal fact." It does so in a way that is as moving as it is controlled. In six short lines, the simplest of words are assembled with the aid of one rhyme for profile (lines 2 and 6); word repetition (line 1; lines 4–5) for intensity; contrast (as indicated above) for focus. The title, appropriately, is both simple and pregnant with connotations. At first glance, one may be inclined to take "Lines" to be a nondescript, humble announcement of some humble poetic lines. Having read these, the "lines" marking an aging face will enter into one's mental picture, and together with them, and most importantly, the facial lines caused by, and giving expression to, grief. These connotations will subsequently enrich one's understanding of the title. Its deceptive simplicity appears to herald aptly the deceptive simplicity of this great little poem. "Nothing more need be said."

Working under considerable physical and mental strain, Bauer in the last year(s) of his life wrote poetry that suggests that the "remoulding" he kept urging himself to undertake had indeed begun. The "radical turn" he had announced to himself seems to have directed his attention away from outer structures towards inner qualities; away from striving for an effective arrangement of his building blocks towards a greater reliance on what these blocks themselves have to offer. As a result, a simple and concise poetic idiom is favoured, one that is richly suggestive, often ambiguous and always strikingly lyrical in tone. These features seem to reflect the "changed heart" of the aging poet who has lost the assurance of younger years and as a result tends to express rather than communicate, and to embrace and offer his art as a means of transcending what darker facts it is obliged to record. The conclusion to be drawn from these observations is best rendered in Bauer's own words: "When no one thought he would do anything worthwhile – he came into his own."

Postscript

♩ *"Hatte es sich gelohnt?*
Gewiß."

"Die zweite Erschaffung der Welt. Das ist die Auszeichnung, die du empfangen hast," Bauer wrote in his diary on 13 April 1958, giving voice to a sense of mission he shared with many fellow artists. The distinction, gratefully received, was at the same time a life sentence to hard labour: "Von großen Leuten lesen – und wie sie schufteten – yes sir," 10 April 1958). The fruits of Bauer's lifelong hard labour are contained in volume upon volume of prose and poetry, varying greatly in kind, length, and interest. Any critical approach to Bauer's œuvre is faced with the daunting task of selection. In attempting to present an overview of his poetry, this study could draw on his own representative choice collected in his parting volume *Lebenslauf*. It provides all the material needed to form an idea of his poetry as a whole, of what remained constant and what was subject to change. Bauer's basic and supreme goal always was to write "human poetry": poetry that speaks to people – to the humane heart and conscience, not to the abstracting or aestheticising intellect. The specific themes he chose for doing this were taken from his immediate surroundings and experiences, and they addressed issues that drew his attention as he continued on his geographical, social, and intellectual travels. At the centre stood always the human being – object of his deeply compassionate criticism and concern. The wide variety of forms Bauer crafted to convey his messages to his fellow man testifies to his serious commitment to, and often effective use of, the poetic medium. While already in his earliest productions there is evidence of considerable skill and effectiveness, the poems of his later years betray a marked tendency towards an expressive efficiency and power that held promise of truly "great" poetry. All the more reason to regret that Bauer's life ended before he had a chance to fulfill this promise.

While the overview presented in these pages could conveniently concentrate on one anthology, any specific study that may be undertaken in the future will have to consult in much greater detail the numerous volumes of poetry, published and unpublished. A collected edition would be a helpful tool. A welcome step in this direction was undertaken recently by Günter Hess and Jürgen Jankofsky who published a *Walter-Bauer-Lesebuch* titled *Sonnentanz* (1996) which offers a well prepared selection of poetry and short prose writings, together with two short essays by Hans-Martin Pleßke and Henry Beissel on "Walter Bauer in Deutschland" (214–19) and "Walter Bauer in Kanada" (220–7) respectively. Intended to reach "new readers for this unjustly forgotten author" (5), this handsome volume serves a worthy cause indeed. It does not, however, fill the place of a complete collection yet to be prepared. This latter, wholly justified by the quality and significance of Bauer's poetry, would be a well deserved, if belated gesture of appreciation – regardless of what Bauer, both as a poet and a literary scholar, felt moved to say about literary scholarship: "I read that they write more books <u>about</u> literature than literature itself. They will talk literature to death ... Everything dies, including B's novels, dramatic pieces, poems. Literature about literature: the tombstone that is lowered on life."[1]

Bauer here voiced a concern that has been raised by members of the creative guild and serious students of literature alike. Yet his own case may serve as an example to show that the reverse may also be true. His own literature could not assert itself because of adverse intellectual-historical and related personal-biographical factors. He refused to swim with the tide of his time, and literary scholarship, carried by currents in spite of its efforts to arrive at objective critical judgment, sealed the lid on the tomb of Bauer's writings by its concerted silence. Recent publications on the poet's life and work appear to have started the long overdue process of lifting the lid and exposing afresh this entombed body of literature and enabling the reader to reach a fair understanding and evaluation of it. It is hoped that the present study of Walter Bauer's poetry may contribute in some small way to this worthwhile project.

Notes

INTRODUCTION

1 "Ich fühlte immer mehr und bedrückend bis zur Verzweiflung, daß ich in eine Sackgasse ging. Ich kam mir fast lächerlich vor mit dem, was ich glaubte und für richtig hielt, wenn ich sah, wie ringsum in Westdeutschland die alten politischen und "geistigen" Kräfte, die wir nie wieder sehen wollten, mit den Gesichtern von Unschuldigen und als durch die Geschichte Bestätigte die Plätze einnahmen ... Ich ertrug die hysterische Überschätzung von Scheinwerten nicht mehr ... Ich sah mich in einem Netz papierner Literaturmacherei gefangen. Ich hatte keinen Atem mehr. Am Ende dessen, was ich durchdachte, war ich mir zu schade, um in der allgemeinen Stickluft ein verbitternd alter Schriftsteller zu werden, der in den Sand schreibt. Ich wollte für mich ein paar Wahrheiten retten, die ich mühsam gefunden und für die ich einiges bezahlt hatte." (*Der Weg zählt* 315)

2 His various prose-writings seem to have fared better than his poetry. For a record of his substantial publications see Riedel, *Wanderer* 219–26.

3 "Diese Eigenart gibt den Arbeiten eine gute, gesunde 'Trockenheit,' ohne daß sie durch übergroße Sprödigkeit der Mitteilung ausgezeichnet wären ... Das heute so oft verdächtige Wort von der literarischen Anständigkeit kommt einem immer wieder bei der Lektüre in den Sinn ... Sie hat eine eigenartige Selbstgenügsamkeit, die sie ohne jede Scheu zeigt. Erfreulich, daß es so etwas in Jahren durchintellektualisierter lyrischer Erzeugnisse noch gibt!" (Krolow 118–19)

4 "Denn es wirkt ja tröstlich, daß ein so gelassen vernünftiger Mann noch immer in der Sprache schreibt, die uns erreicht. Schließlich brauchen wir Stimmen wie diese, jetzt nötiger als zuvor" (Walter 516).

5 "Vielleicht schafft es der im Alter von zweiundsiebzig Jahren in Toronto Verstorbene, mit seinen wichtigsten Arbeiten nun und für immer wieder 'einzuwandern'" (Hagelstange 198).

6 "Und wir folgen ihm in den Raum seiner Prosa und seiner Gedichte, in diese kleinen Werke, die das Herz öffnen den Gedanken der Brüderlichkeit und Solidarität ... die uns der Autor in dieser Prosa von unglaublicher Sensibilität und Genauigkeit erleben läßt" (Trampe 115–16).

7 "Der vorliegende Band zum 90. Geburtstag des Schriftstellers will ... dazu beitragen, aus verschiedenen Sehweisen seine Dichtungen zu erläutern und den zu unrecht Vergessenen ins rechte Licht zu rücken" (Riedel, *Wanderer* 4).

8 "Woran er denke, / Wenn er nachts schlaflos liege? – / ... / Manchmal an einen jungen Menschen, unbekannt, der / Eines Tages vielleicht lesen wird, was ich schrieb.'" ("Interview mit einem älteren Mann," *FH* 92: IX, lines 1–2; 11–12)

9 See Riedel, "Walter Bauers Künstler-Porträts" and "Walter Bauer in seinen Biographien," *Wanderer* 71–83; 84–101.

10 "Morgens schrieb ich ein paar Verse. Gleichviel, ob sie gut oder schlecht sind ... Sie bedeuten mir Atemzüge, und zu wissen, daß ich atme, noch atme, macht mich froh" (*EJ* 149).

CHAPTER ONE

1 "Natürlich sagte ich Herrn Hahnfeld nicht, daß ich schon ganze Schulhefte vollgeschrieben hatte, Gedichte und dramatische Szenen, und auch eine Kunstsammlung hatte ich in einer Mappe angelegt" (*GP* 125–6).

2 "Und so sagte ich denn zu meiner Mutter ... ich sei Manns genug. Ich sagte 'Manns genug,' weil ich den Ausdruck irgendwo gelesen hatte, und er gefiel mir; bei uns zu Hause lachten sie oft über die Ausdrücke, die ich gebrauchte ... 'Nun hören Sie sich das mal an,' sagte meine Mutter, 'der Dreikäsehoch, und was der für Deutsch redet, wie'n Pastor,' und sie lachte, und dabei zog sie mir den alten Hut, den ich aufhatte, übers Gesicht" (*GP* 67–8).

3 "In der Aue bei Merseburg, in der Dämmerung, tropfte es aus dem Himmel, Zeile um Zeile. – Der Mond hat lange ausgeruht von seiner letzten Reise / Er steigt wie aus dem Mund geblasen rund empor ... Ich rannte nach Hause, um es aufzuschreiben, am Küchentisch. The lump in the throat, der Kloß in der Kehle – dabei ist es immer geblieben, auch als ich solche Dinge schrieb wie 'Wenn wir erobern die Universitäten' ... Naiv? Ich gebe es zu" (*EJ* 170).

4 "Auch Brecht kann mir nicht weismachen, daß er kalt wie eine Gurke war, wenn er Verse schrieb. Ich bin etwas mißtrauisch, wenn Poeten lang und breit über die Entstehung eines Gedichtes dozieren – 'Mein Gedicht sei ein Messer,' hieß einmal ein Buch, es war fast lachhaft, wie da

begabte Leute nur von Kälte, von der Absicht, vom Plan schrieben; Ähnliches tun junge Poeten, nicht die besten, in Ostdeutschland" (*EJ* 171)

5 "Der Bewegung folgen Arbeit und Kontrolle der Arbeit" (*LL* 12).

6 "Ein Gedicht ist natürlich kein Gottesgeschenk – old hat, was du da sagst – es ist Arbeit" (*EJ* 170).

7 "Wie kommt es, daß die moderne Literatur den Geschmack des Brotes und einfacher Dinge nicht mehr kennt? Es wird beschrieben, genau, übergenau, aber es ist duftlos, Laboratorium" (*EJ* 144).

8 "Vom Essen und Trinken und der Freude daran ist in der heutigen Literatur kaum die Rede … Keine Zeit zum Essen und Trinken. Man ist zu eifrig damit beschäftigt, die Absurditäten des Lebens zu durchwühlen … Essen sie nie? Trinken sie nie? Rülpsen sie nie? Nein. Das Leben ist zu absurd" (*EJ* 176).

9 "Ich setze auf die Generation der deutschen Germanisten – wenn sie die esoterische Ausflucht des New Criticism vermeidet und nicht nur die Zehen vorsichtig in den Strom des Lebens streckt, von dem Literatur ein Teil ist" (*EJ* 138).

10 "Eines Tages, ihr vom Detail Besessenen, muß man aufhören, die Wellen des Flusses zu zählen, um zu wissen, was der Fluß ist. Das ist der Augenblick der Geburt des Künstlers: er schreitet durch den Fluß oder schwimmt darin und sagt: Wasser, Erde, Fluß, Himmel" (*EJ* 191).

11 "Strengt euch auf eure Weise an. Verwerft die billigen Lösungen. Seid authentisch" (*EJ* 63).

12 "Verse von einem Schweizer Poeten. Alles die gleiche Handschrift. Sentimentalität der Nüchternheit; auch das kann zur Pose werden. Wie lange kann man mit halblauter Stimme reden? Die Sprache besitzt Stolz, Freude, Flügel. Eines Tages muß die Buß- und Bettagverfassung abgeworfen werden. – Schönheit ist nicht Schönschrift." (*EJ* 190)

13 "Es ist wahr: in den vergangenen zwanzig Jahren haben die deutschen Poeten das Wunder der Existenz wiederentdeckt. Doch mir scheint es, als ob in dieser Entdeckung etwas fast ganz fehle – nennen wir es: Mitmensch, Freund, Bruder; nennen wir das Gefühl Freundschaft, Freundlichkeit, Sympathie. Ohne die Gegenwart des Menschen mag die Dichtung glänzen und kühn experimentell sein; aber die Essenz wird ihr fehlen; zuletzt wird sie aufhören, Dichtung zu sein" (*EJ* 72).

14 "Jetzt sind so viele so clever. Sie wissen so viel, daß sie nicht wissen, wo das Herz sitzt" (*EJ* 63).

15 "Goethe glaubte an das menschliche Herz. Tat es nicht auch Brecht – trotz allem?" (*EJ* 89).

16 "Mir saß ein Würgen in der Kehle. Die großen Schriftsteller haben sich nie von der Wirklichkeit entfernt; sie entdeckten die Menschlichkeit noch in einem Hunde" (*EJ* 184).

17 "Das Verhältnis vieler Deutscher zu ihren Schriftstellern ist grund-
falsch, weil es nicht natürlich ist. Sie erwarten Botschaften von ihm,
statt einen Arbeiter auf seinem Felde anzuhören, der zu ihnen sagt: Das
ist es, was ich versucht habe, zu machen" (*EJ* 186).

18 "Das Erwachen des Poeten ist das Erwachen der Morgenröte. Er nimmt
das Licht in die Hand und verteilt es gerecht ... Gerechte Verteilung
des Lichtes ist leicht. Gerechte Verteilung des Brotes ist beträchtlich
schwerer. Dafür muß man unter Umständen seinen Kopf hinhalten"
(*EJ* 193).

19 "Kunst ist Alchemie: eine Chemie höherer Stufe. Sie setzt den Prozeß
des Lebens fort und sublimiert ihn ... denn die Menschen wirken auf-
einander wie Säuren, Salze und Schwefel; alles wirkt aufeinander; in
diesem Prozeß wird der Stoff des Menschenlebens verwandelt und
erhöht. Er wird aufbereitet in Schmerz, in Weisheit, in Liebe" (*EJ* 133).

20 "Man muß einen 'record' zurücklassen. Etwas wie: ich war bei euch,
und das ist mein Bericht" (*EJ* 102).

21 "Daraus wuchs, langsam und nicht ohne Rückfälle, tätige Skepsis, die
bei allem Wissen um die Möglichkeiten und Unmöglichkeiten der
menschlichen Natur von abwägender Sympathie erwärmt wird"
(*LL* 8).

22 "Ich halte es noch immer mit der Bemerkung von Albert Camus, daß
am Menschen mehr zu bewundern als zu verachten ist; obgleich ich
manchmal schlucken muß" (*LL* 8).

CHAPTER SIX

1 "Das Gutgemeinte erweist sich als literarisch armselig. Die Hysterie ist
erschreckend. Soll ich daran teilnehmen? Soll ich mich davon anstecken
lassen? *Diese* Solidarität der Schriftsteller ist dünn gebaut; ... Ich bin ein
Fremder und kann und muß aus dem Fremdsein Reichtum gewinnen.-
Noch immer bin ich bestürzt über die Dürftigkeit und Hysterie. Deut-
sche werden *persönlich*" (1. Mai 1958).

2 "Es war schauerlich ... <u>Warum ist es so schwer, mit Deutschen zusam-
menzusein</u> – Deutschen dieser Art. Zwischen Parzifal und Parade-
schritt ist bei den Deutschen nichts ... Keine Humanität. Diese
unsägliche Schwerfälligkeit. Diese Rivalität, in die ich, ein Fremder,
sofort gezogen wurde. Dieses Gemisch von Hilflosigkeit, Angabe und
Verlogenheit. Dieses Ungeformtsein" (12. Mai 1958).

CHAPTER SEVEN

1 "Ein Mann des achtzehnten Jahrhunderts ... reißt den Grund des Lebens
auf; alles quillt hervor, nur nicht die Schönheit und Liebe. Die Dämonie
von Geiz, Dummheit, Begierde jeder Art tritt die Herrschaft an. In

diesem Werk atmet nicht mehr das achtzehnte Jahrhundert. [Es] …
entsteht *die* Welt, – die Welt aller Zeiten" (*Das Lichte und das Dunkle* 73).

CHAPTER EIGHT

1 "Hatte es sich gelohnt? Gewiß. Jedes Gedicht … enthält einen
geformten Augenblick des Lebens, meines Lebens zu einer gewissen
Zeit. Ich dachte, daß keiner meiner Altersgenossen – sehr viele waren
es nicht mehr – einen solchen Band vorweisen konnte" (*Tagebuch 64*, 23.
Juni 1974).

2 "Ich glaube nicht, daß der Band 'gehen' würde, höchst-wahrscheinlich
kriechen" (12. November 1973; Beissel, UPM 170).

3 "Er [mein Band] wird nicht bemerkt werden. Warum auch eigentlich?
Warum sollte er bemerkt werden – und von wem? Es ist dürres Laub"
(*Tagebuch 65*, 8. Juni 1975).

4 "Aber du hast noch Chancen –: eine Chance. Die radikale Wendung
deines Alters. Gleichviel, was dabei herauskommt. Diese Wendung ist
noch möglich" (*Tagebuch 65*, 8. Juni 1975).

5 "ich selber hänge mir zum Halse heraus. Alles sentimental und ver-
krampft; alles ohne Schwung, ohne Zugriff. Weißt du, wer du bist: ein
alter Mann. Wach auf, Dämmerer – ich bin aufgewacht" (*Tagebuch 64*,
15. Juni 1974).

6 "Ich weiß, was ich für Gedichte schreiben müßte und könnte; aber ich
zögere noch. Zögere nicht zu lange … Männliche Poesie" (*Tagebuch 63*,
12. März 1974).
"Die großen Gedichte kommen noch.––––––––––––––––––
When no one thought he would do anything worthwhile – he came
into his own" (*Tagebuch 63*, 18. April 1974).

7 "Wer aus dem täglichen Leben seiner Sprache herausgetreten ist, muß in
das seiner neuen Sprache eintreten" (*Tagebuch 66*, 27. September 1976).

8 "An einem Konzept von Poesie arbeiten, das die Schärfe von Brecht,
die Urbanität von W.H. Auden, die große, doch nie zerfließende Geste
von St. John Perse vereinigte. Hieße [das] nicht Feuer und Wasser
mischen? Keineswegs" (*Tagebuch 63*, 3. Mai 1974).

9 "Schärfe des Messers; Präzision einer chinesischen Pinselzeichnung –
Präzision muß nicht zu einer Kürze führen, die den Atem erstickt und
tödlich ist" (*Tagebuch 66*, 29. August 1976).

1 "Wie ich lese, werden mehr Bücher <u>über</u> Literatur geschrieben als Lite-
ratur selber. Sie werden Literatur zu Tode reden … Alles stirbt; auch
B's Romane, Stücke, Gedichte. Literatur über Literatur: die Grabplatte,
die sich auf Leben senkt" (*Tagebuch 65*, 23. September 1974).

Works Cited

BAUER'S WORKS

Bauer, Walter. *Kameraden, zu euch spreche ich.* Dresden: Kaden & Co. 1929.
- *Stimme aus dem Leunawerk. Verse und Prosa.* Berlin: Malik 1930. Reissued with a "Nachwort" by Hans-Martin Pleßke. Leipzig: Reclam 1980.
- *Das Lichte und das Dunkle. Bildnisse Europäischer Maler.* Dessau: Karl Rauch 1940.
- *Tagebuchblätter aus Frankreich.* Dessau: Karl Rauch 1941, 1943.
- *Gast auf Erden. Gedichte.* Dessau: Karl Rauch 1943.
- *Tagebuchblätter aus dem Osten.* Dessau: Karl Rauch 1944.
- "Botschaften." Unpublished poems. 1944–6.
- *Dämmerung wird Tag. Gedichte.* Kassel: Harriet Schleber 1947.
- *Die zweite Erschaffung der Welt. Ein europäisches Lesebuch.* Recklinghausen: Bitter 1947, 1948.
- "Tagebuch aus Kanada." Heft 1–66 (1952–76). Unpublished Manuscript. Deutsches Literaturarchiv, Marbach am Neckar.
- *Nachtwachen des Tellerwäschers. Gedichte.* München: Desch 1957.
- *Klopfzeichen. Gedichte.* Hamburg: Tessloff 1962.
- *Der Weg zählt, nicht die Herberge.* Hamburg: Tessloff 1964.
- "German Poetry Today." *University of Toronto Quarterly.* 34: 3 (April 1965): 205–25.
- *Fragment vom Hahnenschrei. Gedichte.* Hamburg: Merlin 1966.
- *Ein Jahr. Tagebuchblätter aus Kanada.* Hamburg: Merlin 1967.
- *The Price of Morning. Selected Poems.* Translated, edited and with an introduction by Henry Beissel. Vancouver/Victoria: Prism International 1968.
- *Lebenslauf. Gedichte 1929 bis 1974.* München: Desch 1975.
- *A Different Sun.* Translated from the German by Henry Beissel. Ottawa: Oberon 1976.

- "Eight Poems Written in English," edited by Henry Beissel. *The Tamarack Review* 77/8 (Summer 1979): 25–34.
- "From the Last Years of his Diary." Selected and translated by Henry Beissel. *The Tamarack Review* 77/8 (Summer 1979): 40–59.
- *Geburt des Poeten. Erinnerungen.* Frankfurt am Main: Suhrkamp 1980.
- *Sonnentanz. Ein Walter-Bauer-Lesebuch.* Ed. Günter Hess and Jürgen Jankofsky. Halle (Saale): projekte verlag 188, 1996.

CRITICAL LITERATURE

Arend, Angelika. "Beissel's Bauer. Some Comments on a Poet's Translation Work." *Seminar* 26 (1990): 34–51.

Beissel, Henry. "Der Atem und das Licht: The Unpublished Manuscripts of Walter Bauer's Last Decade." In: Riedel, *Der Wanderer* 169–95.

- "Walter Bauer in Kanada." In: Hess/Jankofsky, *Sonnentanz* 220–7.

Froeschle, Hartmut. "Walter Bauer. Sein dichterisches Werk mit besonderer Berücksichtigung seines Kanada-Erlebnisses." *Deutschkanadisches Jahrbuch* V (1979): 77–100.

Grupe, Walter. "Ein Dichter aus Merseburg." *Neue deutsche Literatur* 28: 12 (1980): 167–9.

Hagelstange, Rudolf. "Gedenkwort für Walter Bauer." *Jahrbuch Deutsche Akademie für Sprache und Dichtung* (1976): 196–8.

Hess, Günter. "The German Immigrant Writer Walter Bauer. The Burden of his European 'Luggage.'" In: Walter Riedel, ed. *The Old World and the New. Literary Perspectives of German-speaking Canadians,* 59–72. Toronto: University of Toronto Press 1984. Now also in: Riedel, *Der Wanderer* 59–70.

Jankofsky, Jürgen. "'Etwas wie eine *underground reputation*': Wirkungen Walter Bauers auf zeitgenössische Autoren und Künstler seiner mitteldeutschen Heimat." In: Riedel, *Der Wanderer* 163–8.

Krolow, Karl. "Walter Bauer. Klopfzeichen." *Neue deutsche Hefte* 10: 95 (1963): 118–19.

Maczewski, Johannes. "Auf der Suche nach dem NICHTS: Zu Walter Bauers Kanada-Gedichten." *Yearbook of German-American Studies* 19 (1984): 133–53. Now also in: Riedel, *Der Wanderer* 129–52.

Pleßke, Hans-Martin. "Walter Bauer. Vortrag über Leben und Werk." Address given in 1983 in Leipzig. *Deutschkanadisches Jahrbuch* IX (1986): 174–82.

- "'Alles was ist, hat den gleichen Quell': Über das erzählerische Werk von Walter Bauer." In: Riedel, *Der Wanderer* 35–57.

Riedel, Walter. Das literarische Kanadabild: Ein Vergleich zu ausgewählten Werken von Walter Bauer und Henry Beissel." *Deutschkanadisches Jahrbuch* ix (1986): 183–97. – An English adaptation of this essay was published under the title "Silence: Walter Bauer's Myth of the Arctic." In: Riedel, *Der Wanderer* 153-62.

– "Scribo, ergo sum: Walter Bauer, Diarist." *Seminar* 23: 3 (1987): 236–50. – Now also in: *Der Wanderer* 115–28.

– "'Vom Andern und vom Selbst': Walter Bauers Künstler-Porträts." In: *Der Wanderer* 71–83.

– "Walter Bauer in seinen Biographien." In: *Der Wanderer* 85–101.

Riedel, Walter and Rodney Symington, eds. *Der Wanderer. Aufsätze zu Leben und Werk von Walter Bauer.* Frankfurt am Main: Peter Lang 1994.

Symington, Rodney. "The Literature of Voluntary Exile. The German-Canadian Example." In: Burkhardt Krause, Ulrich Scheck, and Patrick O'Neill, eds. *Präludien. Kanadisch-deutsche Dialoge*, 248–63. München: iudicium 1992. Now also under the title "'Bis zum Ende ein fremder Vogel': Walter Bauer and the Dilemma of Exile." In: Riedel, *Der Wanderer* 197–213.

Trampe, Wolfgang. "'Stimme aus dem Leunawerk' von Walter Bauer." *Neue deutsche Literatur* 28: 12 (1980): 112–16.

Hans-Albert Walter. "Eine wichtige Stimme. Walter Bauer: 'Ein Jahr'. Tagebuchblätter aus Kanada." *Frankfurter Hefte* 23 (1968): 514–16.

OTHER WORKS

Bender, Hans, ed. *Mein Gedicht ist mein Messer. Lyriker zu ihren Gedichten.* München: List 1961.

Benn, Gottfried. *Ausgewählte Briefe.* Ed. Max Rychner. Wiesbaden: Limes 1957.

Hage, Volker, ed. *Lyrik für Leser. Deutsche Gedichte der siebziger Jahre.* Stuttgart: Reclam 1980.

Manyoni, Angelika. *Consistency of Phenotype. A Study of Gottfried Benn's Views on Lyric Poetry.* Bern-Frankfurt am Main: Peter Lang 1983.

Index